Adobe Captivate 7 for Mobile Learning

Create mobile-friendly and interactive m-learning content with Adobe Captivate 7

Damien Bruyndonckx

PUBLISHING

BIRMINGHAM - MUMBAI

Adobe Captivate 7 for Mobile Learning

First published: August 2013

Production Reference: 1200813

Published by Packt Publishing Ltd.
Livery Place
35 Livery Street
Birmingham B3 2PB, UK.

ISBN 978-1-84969-955-6

www.packtpub.com

Cover Image by Abhishek Pandey (abhishek.pandey1210@gmail.com)

Credits

Author
Damien Bruyndonckx

Reviewers
Joe Ganci

Anita Horsley

Lieve Weymeis

Acquisition Editor
Kunal Parikh

Commissioning Editor
Harsha Bharwani

Technical Editor
Pratik Vijay More

Project Coordinator
Deenar Satam

Proofreader
Joel T. Johnson

Indexer
Hemangini Bari

Production Coordinator
Kyle Albuquerque

Cover Work
Kyle Albuquerque

Foreword

Smart phones and tablets have changed the way people learn. The power of these nifty gadgets is helping them move from formal learning to an anytime and anywhere learning environment. The spike in the trends of "Just in Time" and "On Demand" learning have also increased the demand for deploying learning snacklets to mobile devices.

These trends have made it essential for e-learning professionals to learn how to create m-learning courses. As always, there are different people with different requirements. Some want to create mobile learning courses, specifically designed for mobile devices. Some want to reuse existing e-learning courses and transform them to m-learning courses, and there are others who wish to make their existing e-learning courses available on mobile devices as well.

Adobe Captivate 7 is a rapid authoring tool, which allows the authors to create simulations, compliance training courses, scenario-based courses, video-based courses, process trainings, assessments, and so on. It is now also capable of creating m-learning courses by allowing you to publish your courses in HTML5 format and create web apps.

In this book, Damien has done a great job of explaining how to use Adobe Captivate 7 for creating m-learning courses. He has provided a step-by-step procedure on how to create mobile-friendly screencasts, interactive simulations, and quizzes. He has covered all of the nuances and best practices for optimizing an existing project for mobile, and publishing it as an HTML5 course or a web application.

So, if you are an e-learning professional and have been using Captivate for years for creating e-learning courses, this book will help you easily transition to m-learning development using the very same tool. Happy learning!

Dr Pooja Jaisingh

Adobe e-learning Evangelist

About the Author

Damien Bruyndonckx, trained as an elementary school teacher, began his career teaching French as a foreign language in two elementary public schools of Louisiana, USA. In 2001, he came back to his home country, Belgium, and began to work as an IT trainer. He soon acquired the title of Adobe Certified Instructor on Dreamweaver, Coldfusion, Acrobat, and Captivate, which allowed him to work for various Adobe authorized training centers in Europe, and participate in many web and e-learning related projects for countless customers.

In 2009, Damien went back to teaching in a school. He now works at IHECS, a higher education school of communications, based in Brussels, where he teaches multimedia and serves as the e-learning coordinator of the school. Thanks to his work at IHECS, Damien became an Adobe Education Leader in November 2011.

Damien also has his own company that provides Adobe Training and e-learning consultancy.

Damien is the author of *Mastering Adobe Captivate 6* published by Packt Publishing in August 2012. He lives in Thuin (Belgium) with his girlfriend and his two children. Damien is a big time music lover, and occasionally works as a sound and light technician in the entertainment industry.

Twitter: @damienbkx

Website: http://www.dbr-training.eu

Acknowledgement

With the release of this book, a new adventure comes to an end. This one was made of hard work, heavy thinking, and deep moments of doubts. But, as with every adventure in life, it was also made of great collaboration, encounters and love. At the end of the road, when you finally hold the book in your hands, you only remember those great people you worked with and who dedicated part of their time and expertise to the project.

I would like to thank my editors at Packt Publishing for their continuous support and mentoring during the entire writing process. Harsha and Deenar, knowing that you were just an e-mail away was really reassuring for me. Many thanks to you!

I would also like to recognize the work of my reviewers. Anita, Lieve, and Joe are among the greatest Captivate minds I know. It was an honor to have them onboard this project. They have my deep appreciation for the work done with this book and with the entire Captivate community.

Speaking of the community, I would like to recognize the work of those individuals that spend some of their free time writing Captivate tutorials, blog posts, forum replies, and so on. These boys and girls have been my real Captivate teachers, and without their input, I would never have been able to become a Captivate expert. I dedicate this book to all those who make the Captivate community a very active, focused, and truly knowledgeable community.

My thoughts also go to the Captivate team in India that is working really hard to create and enhance Captivate on a daily basis. Special thanks to Allen, Pooja, Vish, Shammeer, Akshay, and to everyone else in their respective teams. I have full respect for the work they are doing.

Finally, my thoughts go to those who share my life on a daily basis. They had to cope with my insane working hours and my "out of this world" preoccupations while I was writing this book. Thanks you Celine, Antoine, and Sophie for your patience and understanding. I couldn't do it without you all.

About the Reviewers

Joe Ganci is an e-learning consultant with a long track record. Since 1983, Joe's design approaches and his expert use of development tools have helped many to improve their e-learning design and development. Joe's personal and hands-on style has his services constantly in demand, and he is privileged to have visited many clients all over the world. He has taught people for many years at client sites, and has taught at many learning conferences, where he has often served as a keynote speaker. Joe is on a mission to improve the quality of e-learning with practical approaches that work.

Joe and his team designs and develops e-learning applications from start to finish, from analysis to evaluation, and assist at every level in between. He is a renowned trainer of development tools everywhere in the world, and collaborates with tool vendors to help bridge the gap between design needs and tool offerings.

Joe can be found at his site www.elearningjoe.com, where you will also find many useful tools to assist you in your own e-learning needs.

Joe has four books on e-learning development, more coming.

Anita Horsley is passionate about all forms of teaching and education. She has been a teaching instructor and has led train-the-trainer courses since 1998. As a firefighter, she was a state and national level Instructor III and as a personal trainer, she received train-the-trainer fitness certification through AFFA and IFA. As the Training and Development Specialist for the Oregon State Fire Marshal, she implemented, from inception, the eLearning track and has been designing and developing eLearning courses for adult learners since 2009. She has a Masters degree in Education and is an Adobe Certified Expert in Captivate.

Currently, she is the founder and president of CALEX Learning Consultants. She also works with Engage Systems teaching Adobe Captivate to local and state government agencies and is an adjunct instructor for Portland Community College. She is an author for Packt Publishing, having published Fast Track to Adobe Captivate 6 - a tutorial course with forty 3 to 5 minute videos that teaches the fundamentals of using Adobe Captivate.

She also provides one-on-one online instructions for Adobe Captivate. Horsley is even a presenter on eLearning and Adobe Captivate at conferences nationally.

Simultaneously, Horsley writes a blog, Crazy About Captivate, which provides written and video tutorials on Adobe Captivate. She also provides webinars for ASTD and Adobe. She is a technical reviewer for Packt Publishing as well. Horsley works with the Charleston Animal Society teaching elementary schools kids about the humane treatment to animals and volunteers at Charleston Area Therapeutic Riding, working with kids who have various disabilities but riding horses.

CALEX Learning Consultants, LLC provides technology-based training solutions to business, local, and state agencies. We provide creative eLearning project design, course/curriculum development, and management of education efforts that are focused on customers' direct goals. Additionally, we train customers on how to build eLearning through the use of Adobe Captivate offering one-on-one web-based instructions and group instructor-led training. Simultaneously, we provide consultation, project planning, and deployment.

Our key focus is to develop exceptional engaging and interactive adult educational programs that positively affect agency goals and objectives.

Lieve Weymeis is a civil engineer and professional musician. After years of research in stability of shell constructions, she started as a college lecturer in departments of Construction/Real Estate, teaching several technical courses and ICT. In Flanders, she is known as a specialist in project management, blended learning, and e-learning. As head of the Department of Construction, she introduced new pedagogical methodologies.

Presently she is doing research work on blended learning, e-learning, and social media; developing e-learning courses and trains in Photoshop, Indesign, Captivate, and Presenter.

As a beta-tester, she was invited to be a member of the Advisory Board for Captivate in 2009. In 2011 she became an AEL and ACE, and was granted an Impact award. She is an active member of the Captivate Community on the user forums, Twitter and Linkedin.

She presented several webinars for Adobe, and sessions/workshop at DevLearn 2011 and 2012. Her blog http://blog.lilybiri.com is a reference for worldwide Captivate users.

www.PacktPub.com

Support files, eBooks, discount offers and more

You might want to visit www.PacktPub.com for support files and downloads related to your book.

Did you know that Packt offers eBook versions of every book published, with PDF and ePub files available? You can upgrade to the eBook version at www.PacktPub.com and as a print book customer, you are entitled to a discount on the eBook copy. Get in touch with us at service@packtpub.com for more details.

At www.PacktPub.com, you can also read a collection of free technical articles, sign up for a range of free newsletters and receive exclusive discounts and offers on Packt books and eBooks.

http://PacktLib.PacktPub.com

Do you need instant solutions to your IT questions? PacktLib is Packt's online digital book library. Here, you can access, read and search across Packt's entire library of books.

Why Subscribe?

- Fully searchable across every book published by Packt
- Copy and paste, print and bookmark content
- On demand and accessible via web browser

Free Access for Packt account holders

If you have an account with Packt at www.PacktPub.com, you can use this to access PacktLib today and view nine entirely free books. Simply use your login credentials for immediate access.

Table of Contents

Preface

Since October 2004 and the release of Macromedia Captivate1, Adobe Captivate has always been the industry leading solution for authoring professional SCORM compliant e-learning content. With the advent of mobile devices, the entire e-learning industry has had to adapt. Our students use new devices, new pedagogical opportunities are yet to be fully investigated and authoring tools give us new possibilities.

As of Adobe Captivate 6, it is now possible to publish our courses in HTML5 format, effectively enabling mobile content publishing with Adobe Captivate.

This book takes you through the process of creating and publishing e-learning content for mobile devices. The sample files and the step-by-step instructions have been designed to walk you through the process of creating new content for various mobile devices, and optimizing existing content for mobile devices. This book also covers the creation of quizzes and the publication of the content in HTML5.

Thanks to Adobe Captivate 7 for Mobile Learning, you'll make your e-learning content available to all your students, regardless of the devices they are using.

What this book covers

Chapter 1, Creating a Mobile Compliant Screencast, will show you how to use the Video Demo recording mode of Captivate to create a high-definition screencast. You will then publish your work as a .mp4 file which can be played back on any desktop and mobile device.

Chapter 2, Creating a Mobile-friendly Interactive Simulation, will take you through the steps for creating a typical Captivate interactive simulation. You will create that project with mobile devices in mind and use the mobile-friendly features and objects of Captivate.

Chapter 3, Optimizing an Existing Project for Mobile, starts with an existing Captivate project. Your task is to optimize it for mobile devices. This includes finding the features used in the project that are not supported in HTML5, and replacing them with mobile-friendly features.

Chapter 4, Creating a Mobile-friendly Quiz, focuses on making a quiz, ready for publication in HTML5. You will learn how to create a SCORM manifest file to enable data tracking by an LMS.

Chapter 5, Publishing a Captivate Project for Mobile, teaches you how to make your projects available to the outside world by publishing them. You will explore the HTML5 publishing capabilities of Captivate 7, and take a close look at the generated HTML, CSS, and JavaScript files.

Chapter 6, The Adobe Captivate App Packager, explores two new features brought by the Adobe Captivate App Packager. The first one is importing Edge Animate animations into Captivate. The second one is using the PhoneGap Build service to package your projects as native mobile applications for various mobile operating systems, including iOS and Android.

What you need for this book

- Adobe Captivate 7, a free 30-day trial can be downloaded from the Adobe website at www.adobe.com (most exercises can be done with Adobe Captivate 6 also).

- An HTML5 compliant web browser.

- Adobe Edge Animate that is available as part of a Creative Cloud subscription. A 30-day trial is available on the Adobe website at www.adobe.com. This is optional.

Who this book is for

This book has been primarily written for teachers, instructional designers, professors, curriculum experts, subject matter experts, and e-learning developers wanting to provide mobile-friendly content to their audience.

A basic knowledge of your operating system is required to follow the exercises of this book. No prior knowledge of Captivate is required, although some experience with Captivate is an asset.

Conventions

In this book, you will find a number of styles of text that distinguish between different kinds of information. Here are some examples of these styles, and an explanation of their meaning.

Code words in text are shown as follows: "Captivate is able to insert video files with the extensions `.flv`, `.f4v`, `.avi`, `.mp4`, `.mov`, and `.3gp`."

New terms and **important words** are shown in bold. Words that you see on the screen, in menus or dialog boxes for example, appear in the text like this: "Click on the **Record** button at the bottom-right corner of the recording window".

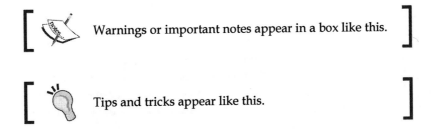

Warnings or important notes appear in a box like this.

Tips and tricks appear like this.

Reader feedback

Feedback from our readers is always welcome. Let us know what you think about this book—what you liked or may have disliked. Reader feedback is important for us to develop titles that you really get the most out of.

To send us general feedback, simply send an e-mail to feedback@packtpub.com, and mention the book title via the subject of your message.

If there is a topic that you have expertise in and you are interested in either writing or contributing to a book, see our author guide on www.packtpub.com/authors.

Customer support

Now that you are the proud owner of a Packt book, we have a number of things to help you to get the most from your purchase.

Errata

Although we have taken every care to ensure the accuracy of our content, mistakes do happen. If you find a mistake in one of our books—maybe a mistake in the text or the code—we would be grateful if you would report this to us. By doing so, you can save other readers from frustration and help us improve subsequent versions of this book. If you find any errata, please report them by visiting `http://www.packtpub.com/submit-errata`, selecting your book, clicking on the **errata submission form** link, and entering the details of your errata. Once your errata are verified, your submission will be accepted and the errata will be uploaded on our website, or added to any list of existing errata, under the Errata section of that title. Any existing errata can be viewed by selecting your title from `http://www.packtpub.com/support`.

Piracy

Piracy of copyright material on the Internet is an ongoing problem across all media. At Packt, we take the protection of our copyright and licenses very seriously. If you come across any illegal copies of our works, in any form, on the Internet, please provide us with the location address or website name immediately so that we can pursue a remedy.

Please contact us at `copyright@packtpub.com` with a link to the suspected pirated material.

We appreciate your help in protecting our authors, and our ability to bring you valuable content.

Questions

You can contact us at `questions@packtpub.com` if you are having a problem with any aspect of the book, and we will do our best to address it.

1
Creating a Mobile Compliant Screencast

Everything started in 2007 when Apple launched the first iPhone. This event was the kick off of the mobile revolution. Right from the start, Apple chose not to support the Flash player on their iOS devices. In November 2011, Adobe announced that they would no longer develop the mobile version of the Flash player. The entire industry would need to switch from Adobe Flash technology to HTML5 standards.

 See Steve Jobs's thoughts on Flash at the URL `http://www.apple.com/hotnews/thoughts-on-flash/` and Adobe's announcement on Flash player for mobile at the URL `http://blogs.adobe.com/conversations/2011/11/flash-focus.html`.

Adobe Captivate was built on top of the Flash technology, which allowed Captivate to produce highly interactive e-learning content. With the rising popularity of non-Flash devices and the focus shifting from Flash to HTML5, a major change was needed for Adobe Captivate. Don't underestimate the significance of this change! Adobe Flash is in the DNA of Adobe Captivate, so shifting from Adobe Flash to HTML5 is like creating entirely new software!

Captivate 7 was released in June 2013, and contains a variety of new features that help e-learning developers address the mobile challenge. We will cover these features in detail throughout this book.

In this first chapter, we will:

- Use Video Demo recording to capture onscreen action
- Discuss the typical Captivate production workflow
- Enhance the captured video with two basic objects of Captivate
- Edit an HD video using pan, zoom, and transitions
- Publish projects as a `.mp4` video file
- Publish to YouTube

The Video Demo recording mode at a glance

The Video Demo recording mode of Captivate is a special recording mode, entirely dedicated to producing video files (with a `.mp4` file extension). Such a video file can be played back on any desktop and mobile device. It can also be uploaded to online video hosting services, such as YouTube, DailyMotion, or Vimeo.

On the downside, the resulting file is a plain video file which the student experiences from the beginning to the end with no possibility of interaction. That's why the Video Demo authoring environment is a simplified version of Captivate with only a small subset of the features available.

Creating a video screencast

In this chapter, we will create a simple video screencast using the Video Demo recording mode of Captivate. If you've never used Captivate before, this will be a good way to get started and to have a first look at the typical Captivate production workflow. Along the way, we will discuss some of the objects and features available in Captivate 7.

Step zero – the pre-production step

The first step of the typical Captivate production workflow is the pre-production step. It is the only step that does not take place in Captivate, which is the reason why I like to refer to it as step zero.

To me, this is the single most important step of the entire process. It is in this step that you will develop the scenario of your online course. What will you teach your students? In what order will you introduce each topic? When and how will you assess their knowledge? Those are important questions that every single e-learning developer should address prior to opening Captivate for the first time. At the end of this step, you should have some kind of scenario available. This scenario will be your guide during the rest of the production.

In this example that this book offers, the pre-production phase has been done for you. Let's now take a look at the project that we will build together in the next few pages.

 If you did not download the exercise files of this book yet, please do so now.

Perform the following steps once the exercise files of the book have been downloaded:

1. Open Adobe Captivate 7.
2. On the welcome screen, click on the open link.
3. Open the `finished/comePlayWithUs.cpvc` file present in the folder you downloaded from the Packt website.
4. Once the file is open, navigate to the **File | Preview | Full Screen** menu item.

Captivate switches to full screen mode and plays the finished screencast. For this first example, you'll pretend to be the webmaster of **HD Street Band**, a fictional concert band. Your goal is to demonstrate a new feature that you have implemented on the band's website.

While watching the screencast, focus your attention on the objects that are overlaid on top of the video. You will see two smart shapes (the orange rounded rectangle on top of the form and the orange arrow pointing at the **Other** option of the **Instrument** drop-down list), and three text captions (two transparent captions, at the beginning and at the end of the video, and a green caption stating that the e-mail field is required). Images have been inserted at the beginning and at the end of the video, and transitions have been used between these images and the actual video. Finally, a pan and zoom effect is used in the middle video to focus on the **Instrument** drop-down list. Don't hesitate to view this video a few times in order to spot each of the features mentioned.

5. When done, click on the **Edit** button at the bottom-right corner of the screen to return to the editing environment.
6. Use the **File | Close** menu item to close the file without saving the changes.

You should now be back to the welcome screen of Captivate 7.

Step one – the capture step

The capture step is the first step of the typical Captivate production workflow that takes place in Captivate. In this step, you will use the screen capture engine of Captivate to capture the onscreen action. In other words, you will perform the actions you want to record on your computer, and behind the scenes, Captivate will record everything you do.

When capturing the onscreen action, two applications will be open at the same time. The first one is the application that you want to capture, and the second is Adobe Captivate which will be capturing the action. We will now get these two applications ready for the capture session.

Getting the captured application ready

In this case, what we want to capture is a website, so the application to capture is our default web browser.

1. Use the Windows Explorer (Windows) or the Finder (Mac) to go to the `/HDStreet-Site` folder of the sample files and double-click on `index.html`.

The HD Street Band's home page opens in your default web browser.

2. Take some time to explore the website. Pay special attention to the **Come play with us** page.
3. While on the **Come play with us** page, take some time to fill and submit the form. Make sure your computer behaves as expected before the actual recording session.

It is a good idea to test the functionality you want to record before actually recording it. In this case, for instance, an e-mail message is generated when you click on the **Join the band** button. This requires that an e-mail client be correctly configured on your system.

Practice what you're about to record. The actual narration that you will speak out is not important, but for the sake of this exercise, you should perform the actions in the correct order. Refer to the following table to make sure you record all of the material we need to conduct this exercise to the end.

Step	Action	Narration
1	HD Street Band's home page.	Briefly introduce yourself as the band's webmaster. Explain that you have developed a new feature on the site.
2	Go to the **Come play with us** page and scroll down to see the entire form.	State that the new feature is the form on the **Come play with us** page. Briefly explain its purpose.
3	Fill the first and last name fields.	Explain that you are filling the first and last name fields as you do it.
4	Fill the e-mail address field.	Don't forget to specify that the e-mail address is a required information.
5	Open the **Instrument** drop-down list.	Explain the purpose of the **Other** option at the end of the list.
6	Select the instrument of your choice.	Choose any instrument in the list.
7	Type a short comment.	Explain that the **Comments** field allows the future musician to add some more information to its application.
8	Click on the **Join the band** button. Your e-mail client should generate a new e-mail message.	Explain that the body of the e-mail message contains the information typed in the form.
9	Send the e-mail message.	Explain that the last step is to actually send the automatically generated e-mail message.
10	Concluding statement.	Thank the student for watching the video and make a nice closing comment.

The above table is your scenario. Feel free to take a piece of paper and write down the actual narration that you'll record based on the above table. Once you master the scenario, move on to the next steps as described.

4. Click on the **Home** button to return to the HD Street Band's home page, and leave your default browser open on the band's home page.

Your web browser is now ready to be captured. The next step is to get Captivate ready to record your web browser.

Getting Captivate ready for the recording session

We will now return to Captivate and explore the options to record the Video Demo screencast.

 If you plan on recording narration, make sure your audio system is correctly set up before starting this procedure.

Perform the following steps to return to Captivate and explore the options to record the Video Demo screencast:

1. Return to Captivate. Click on the **Video Demo** link situated in the right column of the welcome screen. Alternatively, you can go to the **File | Record new Video Demo** menu item.

The main Captivate interface disappears and the recording window opens in the center of the screen. The recording window serves many purposes. First, it will let us tell Captivate what we want to record.

2. At the top of the recording window, choose to record an **Application**.

The red rectangle that appears on your screen is known as the recording area. Captivate will record any action that takes place inside this red recording area.

3. Open the **Select the window to record** drop-down menu.

This drop-down menu lists all of the applications that are currently open. One of them is your default web browser showing the HD Street Band's home page.

4. Select your default browser in the list of opened applications.

The red recording area resizes and snaps to your browser's window. We will now adjust the size of the red recording area:

5. In the **Snap to** area of the recording window, choose the **Custom Size** option.
6. Open the **Custom** drop-down list and choose the **Apple iPad Landscape (1024 x 672)** preset.

Take some time to review the other available preset sizes. Note that Captivate includes many presets suitable for mobile devices.

7. Open the **Audio** drop-down menu in the last section of the recording window.

8. Choose the microphone you want to use to record the narration. The actual content of this drop-down menu depends on the audio devices installed on your system.

If you don't have a microphone available for this exercise, just leave the **Audio** menu to **No Narration**. You'll have a chance to catch up on narration later on. Some people also find it easier to record the narration separately and import into the project later. In such a case, the **Audio** drop-down menu is left to the **No Narration** option as well.

Make sure your screen looks like the following screenshot before moving on to the next step:

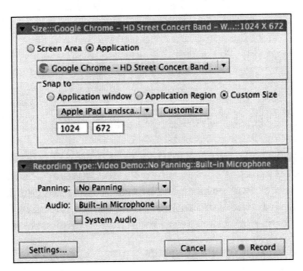

Before moving on to the actual recording, let's review some of the recording options as shown in the following steps:

9. Click on the **Settings** button situated at the bottom left corner of the recording window.

After a short while, the **Preferences** dialog opens.

10. In the left column of the **Preferences** window, click on the **Settings** category.

11. Notice the **Move New Windows Inside Recording Area** checkbox as shown in the following screenshot:

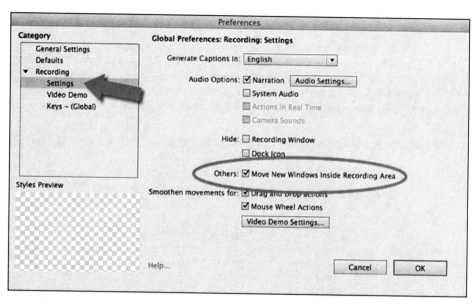

The **Move New Windows Inside Recording Area** option should be selected by default (if not, select it now). It is used when the recorded application opens a new window during the recording session. In our case, the e-mail client will be opened when we click on the **Join the band** button at the end of the form. This option will move the generated e-mail message window inside the red recording area, if needed.

12. In the left column of the **Preferences** dialog, click on the **Keys - (Global)** category.

Remember that when recording a video with Captivate, two applications are running at the same time. This is not a problem for today's operating systems as they all are multitasking systems. That being said, in a normal situation, an operating system only allows one of the running applications to be the active application. The OS wires the mouse and the keyboard to that single active application. Recording a Captivate project is a bit different. Both Captivate and the captured application are active at the same time, and so, we must use the same mouse and keyboard to interact with both applications. To handle this unusual situation, Captivate only listens to the keys and shortcuts listed on the **Keys – (Global)** preferences pane. The rest of the keyboard is wired to the captured application. This allows us to interact with both applications with a single keyboard!

13. Notice the *End* (Windows) key or the *command + Enter* (Mac) shortcut that is used to end the recording.

 You can also end the recording by clicking on the CP icon situated in the notification area of the taskbar (Windows), or in the upper-right corner of the menu bar (Mac) when the recording is in progress.

14. Click on the **OK** button to close the **Preferences** window.

You're now ready to start the actual recording session!

Record the onscreen action

Captivate is ready to capture the onscreen action, our default web browser is ready to be captured by Captivate, we have tested the functionality that we want to record, and we have rehearsed our script. It is time to get to the real stuff and hit the **Record** button:

1. Click on the red **Record** button at the bottom corner of the recording window.

If you have chosen to record the narration, and if you have never recorded narration with Captivate before, you must set the sensitivity of your microphone.

2. Click on the **Auto calibrate** button and say a few words in the microphone (Don't worry! These are not recorded!). This step is optional.

3. When the green **Input level OK** message appears, take a deep breath and click on the **OK** button to start the actual recording! This step is optional.

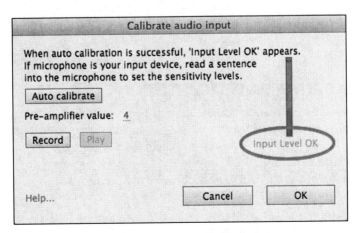

After a short countdown, you'll be in recording mode.

4. Perform all of the actions as rehearsed earlier in this chapter, and speak out everything you do! When done, use the *End* (Windows) or *command + Enter* (Mac) shortcut to stop the recording.

On some Mac models, you must use the *command + fn + Enter* shortcut instead of the *command + Enter* shortcut to stop the recording.

Don't worry if you don't get it right on the first attempt. Just stop the recording, reset your Internet browser to the first step of the scenario and have another try! For your information, it took me six attempts to record the sample video you downloaded from the Internet!

When you have completed the video recording, Captivate displays the **Finalizing video capture** message. This step can take some time depending on the length of the captured video and on the performances of your computer. When finished, Captivate plays the captured video in full screen mode.

5. If you are happy with the captured video, click on the **Edit** button at the bottom-right corner of the screen.

6. Navigate to the **File | Save As** menu item to save the project in your exercises folder. Name it comePlayWithUs.cpvc.

The file extensions used by Captivate
The normal file extension when saving a Captivate project is .cptx, but the Video Demo projects use their own .cpvc file extension.

This is end of the capture step, which is the first step of the typical Captivate production workflow.

Step two – the editing step

This is the most time-consuming step of the entire process. The goal of the editing step is to turn the raw material, provided by the capture step, into e-learning content. This involves tasks such as working with objects (text captions, smart shapes, and so on), applying effects, and using the timeline of Captivate among other things. At the end of the editing step, your course should be ready for publishing.

If you did not succeed in producing a nice raw video during the capture step, or if you did not record the narration, use the comePlayWithUs_raw.cpvc file situated in the exercises folder.

Touring the Video Demo interface

Before we get started, let's take some time to get acquainted with the Captivate interface, as shown in the following screenshot:

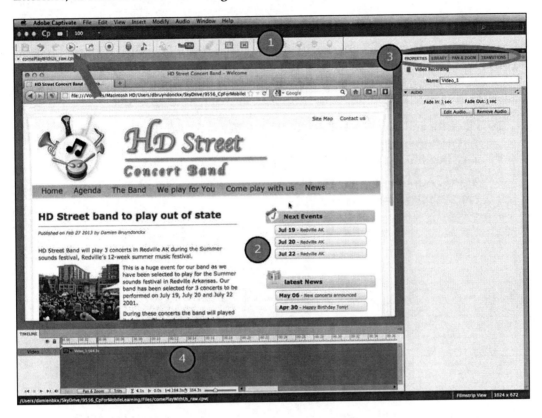

- At the top of the screen is the main options toolbar, marked as **1** in the preceding screenshot. You can hide or show this toolbar by navigating to **Window | Main Options**. The fourth icon of the main options toolbar (shown in the previous screenshot with an arrow) is the Preview icon that we will use to test our video as we build it.
- The main area is called the stage, marked as **2** in the preceding screenshot. This is where you will spend most of your time laying out objects during the editing phase.
- On the right-hand side of the screen are the panels, marked as **3** in the previous screenshot. In the preceding screenshot, the **PROPERTIES** panel is the active one. You can also activate the **LIBRARY**, **PAN & ZOOM**, or the **TRANSITIONS** panels.

- At the bottom of the screen is the **TIMELINE** panel, marked in the preceding screenshot as **4**. We will use it to synchronize the objects that will be inserted in the project with the video and narration.

Trimming the raw video file

Most of the time, you won't get exactly the expected result out of the capture phase, so our first task should be to clean up the video file a little bit. This operation is made very easy, thanks to the **Trim** tool. We will now use the **Trim** tool to remove some material at the very beginning of the video as shown in the following steps:

1. Place the red playhead at the location where you want to remove some material from the video. In this case, make sure the playhead is at the very beginning of the **TIMELINE** panel.

2. At the bottom of the **TIMELINE** panel, click on the small **Trim** button (see the following screenshot):

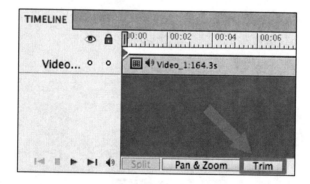

When clicking on the **Trim** button, a small black triangle appears on the **TIMELINE** panel, next to the red playhead. This black triangle can be moved along the **TIMELINE** allowing you to select the portion of the video that you want to trim.

3. Move the black triangle to the right up to the location where the video actually begins. This action effectively selects the first few seconds of the video file.

4. When the required portion of the video is selected, click on the small **Trim** button at the bottom of the **TIMELINE** panel to remove the selected portion of the video.

5. Repeat this procedure for each portion of the video that you want to remove.

The goal of this simple operation is to clean up the raw video file in order to remove any mistakes or imperfections that were captured.

Inserting images

The first object that we will insert in this video is an image at the beginning of the project, accomplished by performing the following steps:

1. Navigate to the **Insert | Image** menu item.
2. Browse to the `images/HDSBTitleTemplate_mobile.png` file located in the exercises folder that you downloaded from the Internet.
3. Import the selected file onto the video.
4. Take a look at the **TIMELINE** panel, at the bottom of the screen. The image has been imported on a second layer above the video. We will now use **TIMELINE** to sync the image with the video.
5. Normally, the image should be the active object. If not, click on the image in the **TIMELINE** panel to make it the active object.
6. Take a look at the **PROPERTIES** panel situated at the right-hand side of the screen.

As in many other Adobe applications, the **PROPERTIES** panel of Captivate is a dynamic panel, which means that it always displays the options pertaining to the selected object.

7. In the **Timing** section of the **PROPERTIES** panel, make the image **Appear after 0 sec.** and **Display For** a **specific time** of **4 sec.**

Note that these changes are reflected in the **TIMELINE** panel.

8. In the **TIMELINE** panel, hover your mouse over the **Video** layer that is at the bottom. The mouse pointer will turn into a grabbing hand.
9. Drag the video to the right to make it begin at 4 sec into the project.

Make sure the **TIMELINE** panel looks like the following screenshot:

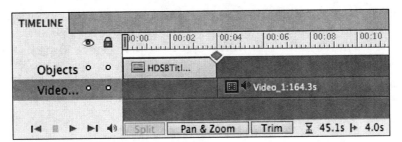

We will now add another instance of the same image at the end of the video:

10. In the **TIMELINE** panel, use the horizontal scroll bar to move to the very end of the project. Click the top-edge of the **TIMELINE** panel to place the playhead (the vertical red bar) at the end of **TIMELINE**.

11. Activate the **LIBRARY** panel situated on the right-hand side of the screen, next to the **PROPERTIES** panel.

Captivate maintains a list of all the external assets (images, sound clips, animations, and so on) inserted into the project in the **LIBRARY** panel.

12. Drag the `HDSBTitleTemplate_mobile.png` file from the **Images** section of the **LIBRARY** panel, onto the stage.

13. Return to the **PROPERTIES** panel and make sure the newly inserted image is selected.

14. In the **Transform** section of the **PROPERTIES** panel, set both the **X** and the **Y** values to 0. This places the image exactly on top of the video.

15. In the **Timing** section of the **PROPERTIES** panel, make the image **Display For** a **specific time** of **4 seconds**.

16. Move the image in the **TIMELINE** panel, so that it begins when the video track ends.

17. Save the file and use the preview icon to preview the video in full screen mode. When done, click on the **Edit** button at the bottom-right corner of the screen to return to the editing environment.

When viewing the video, notice the newly inserted images at the beginning and at the end of the video. In the following section, we will finalize the insertion of these images by adding transitions between the video and the images.

Adding transitions

In a Video Demo project, a transition can be added at the beginning and at the end of a video file as shown in the following steps. Note that a single project can contain multiple video files.

1. In **TIMELINE**, scroll back to the beginning of the project.

2. Click on the small diamond that marks the start of the video file as shown in the following screenshot:

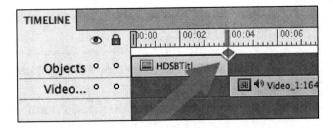

These diamonds are the transition markers. They mark the limits of the video file(s) included the project. When clicking on such a diamond, the **TRANSITIONS** panel opens on the right-hand side of the screen.

3. Choose a transition of your liking from the **TRANSITIONS** panel.
4. Use the horizontal scroll bar of the **TIMELINE** panel to go to the very end of the project.
5. Click on the diamond that marks the end of the video file.
6. In the **TRANSITIONS** panel, choose another transition of your liking in the list of available transitions.

Adding transitions is *that* easy! Don't hesitate to use the preview icon to test your transitions in full screen mode. When done, don't forget to save the file.

Inserting text captions

The text caption object is one of the oldest and most widely used objects of Captivate. Perform the following steps to insert text captions:

1. In the **TIMELINE** panel, move the playhead (the vertical red bar) at **1** second into the project.
2. Navigate to the **Insert | Text Caption** menu item to insert a new text caption at the playhead's position.

Since the image we inserted earlier is still showing at that moment in the **TIMELINE** panel, Captivate places the text caption on top of the image in a new layer.

3. Triple-click into the new text caption to select the entire placeholder text.
4. Type **Come play with us!** into the text caption.
5. Use the *Esc* key to leave the text edit mode and select the text caption object.

Take a look at the **PROPERTIES** panel. Notice that it displays the options of a text caption.

6. In the **Character** section of the **PROPERTIES** panel, change the **Font Family** to **Verdana** and the **Font Size** to **40**.

7. In the **Timing** section of the **PROPERTIES** panel, make the text caption **Appear After 1 sec** and **Display For a Specific Time** of **3 sec**. These changes are reflected on the TIMELINE panel.

8. Make sure the text caption is still selected on the stage and use the resize handle to enlarge the text caption so that the text nicely fits in the container.

9. Move the text caption on top of the lower-right area of the white stripe of the image.

10. In the **Transition** section of the **PROPERTIES** panel, change the transition to **Fade In Only**.

Make sure the TIMELINE panel looks like the following screenshot. When done, save and preview the file.

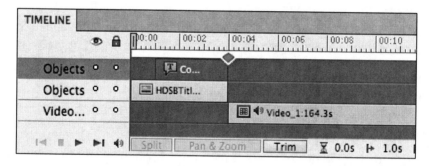

Extra credit

With the techniques you learned in the previous section, insert a second text caption at the very end of the file. These are the general steps to follow:

1. In the **TIMELINE** panel, place the red vertical playhead 3 seconds before the end of the project.

2. Insert a new text caption. Write `Thanks for watching this video` into the new caption.

3. Use the **PROPERTIES** panel to give the new text caption the same formatting properties as the text caption we inserted together.

4. Adjust the size and the position of the new text caption so it fits nicely on top the image.

We will now add a last text caption into the project, and explore some more properties of the text caption object.

Before we get started, notice the five control icons at the bottom-left corner of the **TIMELINE** panel, as shown in the following screenshot. These buttons enable you to control the playback of the video file right from the editing environment of Captivate!

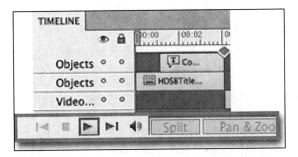

Perform the following steps to insert the last Text Caption of this project:

1. Click on the first icon to move the playhead to the beginning of the file.
2. Click on the Play icon to start playing the movie. Stop the playback when the narration speaks about the required e-mail field.
3. Navigate to the **Insert | Text Caption** menu item to insert a new text caption at the playhead's location. Type **The email field is required** into the new text caption.
4. Use the *Esc* key to leave the text edit mode and select the text caption object.
5. In the **General** section of the **PROPERTIES** panel, open the **Caption** drop-down list and change caption **Type** from **Transparent** to **HaloGreen**.

The text caption on the stage is no longer transparent, but is inserted into a green container. Note that five callout shapes are available for the **HaloGreen** text caption in the **General** section of the **PROPERTIES** panel.

6. Directly below the **Caption** drop-down list, choose the fourth **Callout**.
7. In the **Character** section of the **PROPERTIES** panel, change **Font Family** to **Verdana** and **Font Size** to **40**.
8. In the **Format** section, click on the **Align center** and **Align middle** icons to place the text in the middle of the text caption object.

9. Move and resize the text caption on the stage, so that the text fits nicely into the text caption object, and that the callout points to the **Email** field of the form.

10. Move and resize the object on the **TIMELINE** panel, so it is correctly synchronized with the audio narration and with the video.

11. In the **Transition** section of the **PROPERTIES** panel, change the **Effect** from **No Transition** to **Fade In And Out**.

This exercise illustrates another use of the text caption object. Don't forget to preview and save your file.

Creating a zoom effect

The Video Demo editor makes adding **Pan and Zoom** effects a breeze. In this section, we will use a zoom effect to focus on the **Instrument** drop-down list of the form.

1. Use the buttons at the lower-left corner of the **TIMELINE** panel to play the video file. Stop the playback just before the narration speaks about the **Instruments** drop-down list at the end of the form.

2. Open the **PAN & ZOOM** panel situated in the column at the right-hand side of the screen, next to the **PROPERTIES** panel. Alternatively, click on the **Pan & Zoom** button at the bottom of the **TIMELINE** panel (next to the **Trim** button used earlier).

3. In the **PAN & ZOOM** panel, click on the **Add Pan & Zoom** button to add a zoom effect at the playhead's position (only if you did not use the **Pan & Zoom** button of the **TIMELINE** panel).

4. The default timing of the zoom is at .5 seconds, which means it will zoom in quite fast. Change the timing of the zoom in to about 2 seconds.

5. At the top of the **PAN & ZOOM** panel, resize the blue rectangle in order to focus on the **Instruments** drop-down list. Notice that this manipulation is reflected on the stage.

Make sure your **PAN & ZOOM** panel looks like the following screenshot:

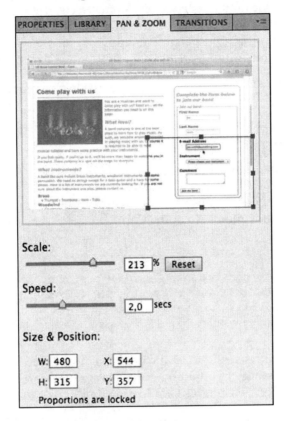

With the zoom in effect in place, we will now focus on adding the reversed, zoom out effect a bit farther in the video:

6. Use the Play button in the lower-left corner of the **TIMELINE** panel to continue playing the video. Stop the playback just before the **Join the band** button is being clicked. This is where we want to add the zoom out effect.

7. In the **PAN & ZOOM** panel, click on the **Zoom Out** button to add a zoom out effect at the playhead's position. If desired, change the timing of the zoom out to about 2 seconds.

In the **TIMELINE** panel, notice two small orange magnifier icons on the video layer. These icons mark the location of our Pan & Zoom effects. If you want to modify such an effect, all you need to do is to click on its magnifier icon to access the effect's properties in the **PAN & ZOOM** panel. To remove a Pan & Zoom effect, right-click on the corresponding magnifier icon and choose **Remove Pan & Zoom**.

Don't forget to preview the video and to save the file before moving on to the next section.

Inserting a smart shape

In this section, we will discuss yet another object of Captivate. A smart shape is a vector object that can be added to a Captivate project and manipulated in many ways. This feature appears in Captivate 6 and offers a great deal of flexibility. It is even considered by many members of the Captivate community as the best new feature of Captivate 6.

 See `http://dbr-training.eu/dbr-Training_en/index.cfm/` `blog/the-real-gems-of-captivate-6/` and `http://` `blog.lilybiri.com/why-i-like-shape-buttons-captivate-6` for more on why smart shapes is the best new feature of Captivate 6.

In our example, we will use a smart shape to highlight the areas of the screen where we want to drive our student's attention. Keep in mind though, that the true power of smart shapes goes far beyond this simple use-case!

1. Use the Play button at the bottom-left corner of the **TIMELINE** panel to play the video file. Stop the playback after the scroll down movement of the video when the entire form is visible on the **Come play with us** page.

2. Navigate to the **Insert | Smart Shape** menu item to open the smart shapes library.

3. In the **Basic** section of the smart shape library, click on the rounded rectangle tool.

4. Click-and-drag your mouse to draw a rounded rectangle on top of the form situated in the sidebar on the right-hand side of the web page.

5. When you release the mouse, the rounded rectangle should be selected.

Notice the yellow square in the top-left corner of the rounded rectangle, which is one of the features that make smart shapes awesome. It allows you to modify the shape itself.

6. Use the yellow square to adjust the roundness of the rectangle so that it roughly matches the roundness of the form's frame.

7. With the rounded rectangle still selected, take a look at the **PROPERTIES** panel.

As expected, the **PROPERTIES** panel shows the properties pertaining to a smart shape object.

8. In the **Fill & Stroke** section of the **PROPERTIES** panel, change **Fill** to an orange shade of your liking.

Note that by default, the fill of a smart shape is a gradient fill. To apply a solid color as the fill, you must first select the solid color icon at the top of the color picker, as shown in the following screenshot:

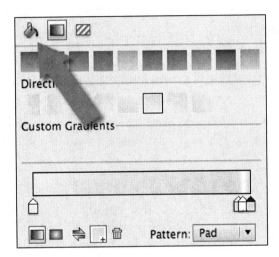

9. Change the opacity to 30 percent.

10. Also change the **Stroke** color to the same orange shade as the fill.

 Use the Eyedropper tool to make sure you're using the very same color.

11. Change the **Width** of the stroke to **3** pixels.

12. In the **Transition** section, change the **Effect** to **Fade In And Out**.

13. In the **TIMELINE** panel, use your mouse to adjust the timing of the smart shape so it plays in sync with the narration and with the video.

Extra credit

Add a second smart shape when the narration talks about the **Other** option of the **Instrument** drop-down list. This second smart shape should be an arrow pointing at the **Other** option of the drop-down list. These are the general steps to follow:

1. Use the controls at the bottom-left corner of the **TIMELINE** panel to spot the correct location.

2. Insert the arrow smart shape. Use the yellow square(s) to adjust the shape if needed. Move and resize the shape to the desired location.

3. Change the **Fill & Stroke** properties of the arrow so they match the **Fill & Stroke** properties of the rounded rectangle you inserted earlier. Use the recent color buttons at the bottom of the swatches panel to make sure you're using the same colors as the previous smart shape.

4. Use the **TIMELINE** panel to adjust the timing of the arrow so it plays in sync with the video and with the narration.

Take a few minutes to preview the entire video in full screen mode and don't forget to save the file.

This is the end of the editing step, which is the second step of the typical Captivate production workflow. In Step 3, you'll learn how to publish your project.

Step three – the publishing phase

The publishing phase is the last phase of the typical Captivate production workflow. The goal of the publishing phase is to make your projects available to the outside world. Captivate is able to publish projects in a variety of formats.

However, a Video Demo project (in other words, a project that uses the .cpvc file extension) can only be published as a .mp4 video file. Any HTML5 compliant browsers (mobile or desktop) should be able to play this video without the need for a third-party plugin.

Publishing as a .mp4 video file

Publishing the Video Demo project as a .mp4 video file is an easy process, as shown in the following steps:

1. Click on the **File | Publish** menu item or on the publish icon situated in the main options toolbar.

2. In the **Publish Video Demo** dialog, make sure the name of the project is **comePlayWithUs**.

3. In the **Folder** field, choose the `published` folder of your exercises as the publish destination.

4. Open the **Preset** drop-down menu, and examine the available presets. Choose the **Video – Apple iPad** preset.

Make sure the Publish Video Demo dialog looks like the following screenshot:

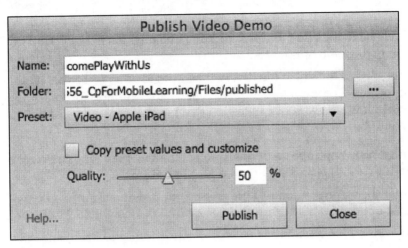

5. Click on the **Publish** button.

Captivate starts the publishing process. The time it takes to publish depends on the length of the video and on the overall performances of your computer system.

6. Click on the **Close** button when the publishing process is complete.

7. Use Windows Explorer (Windows) or the Finder (Mac) to go to the `/published` folder of your exercises.

You should see the `comePlayWithUs.mp4` file that has been generated by Captivate. Double-click on the file to open it in the default video player installed on your system.

This video file can easily be uploaded to a web server and integrated into a web page. If you do not have a website to host your published `.mp4` video, Captivate offers the possibility to upload it to YouTube (www.youtube.com).

Publishing to YouTube

Captivate allows you to upload your Video Demo project to YouTube without leaving the application.

 The following exercise requires that you have a YouTube account and a working Internet connection. If you do not have a YouTube account, you can create one for free at http://www.youtube.com/yt/about/getting-started.html.

1. Navigate to the **File | Publish to YouTube** menu item or click on the **YouTube** icon in the main options toolbar.

Captivate publishes the video file that will be uploaded to YouTube. When the publishing process is complete, Captivate opens the **Adobe Captivate Video Publisher** window, an external application that handles the upload of the published video to YouTube.

2. Enter your YouTube credentials, select the **I've read Adobe Privacy Policy** checkbox and click on the **Log In** button.

3. Enter the video metadata (**Title**, **Description**, and a list of **Tags**), choose the most appropriate **Category** and decide if the video will be **Public** or **Private**.

4. Select the **I have read the terms and conditions** checkbox, and click on the **Upload** button as shown in the following screenshot:

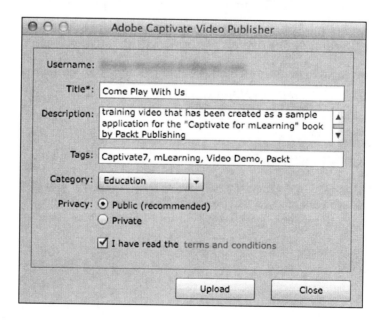

5. Click on the **Close** button to close the **Adobe Captivate Video Publisher** window.

When the upload is complete, the **Adobe Captivate Video Publisher** lets you post the link to your uploaded video on Twitter and Facebook. You can also send the link by e-mail.

Take some time to visit the link to your video using your default web browser. If you have a tablet or a smart phone available, don't hesitate to use your mobile device to view your newly uploaded YouTube content.

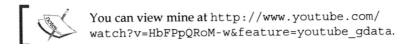 You can view mine at `http://www.youtube.com/watch?v=HbFPpQRoM-w&feature=youtube_gdata`.

Summary

In this chapter, we have explored the Video Demo recording mode of Captivate to produce and publish our first high-definition screencast. The end result of our work is a `.mp4` video file that can be played back on any desktop and mobile device. We also uploaded our video to YouTube, so that we can reach virtually any device connected to the Internet.

You got a lot of things accomplished in a single chapter and that didn't take a lot of time! This demonstrates the leadership of Adobe Captivate as a *rapid* e-learning development tool.

HD video demos are meant for one purpose, they are a "show me" type of file, which means files that are to be watched from the beginning to the end as one single unit. In other words, there is no interactivity possible in this kind of project!

However, the power of Captivate is not limited to producing linear video files! In the next chapter, we will use another recording mode of Captivate to produce interactive e-learning content. Of course, we will make sure that mobile and desktop users can both experience this interactive content in optimal conditions.

2

Creating a Mobile-friendly Interactive Simulation

In this chapter, we will create an interactive virtual tour of the HD street band website. This type of interactive simulation is what Captivate is primarily designed for. In earlier versions of Captivate, this type of project used to be published as an Adobe Flash application (with a .swf file extension). To make it mobile-friendly, we will use the HTML5 publishing format instead.

The end result will be an HTML5 web application. Students will need an HTML5 compliant browser to experience our online course. The good news is that most modern desktop browsers and virtually every mobile browser are HTML5 compliant. This means that our students will be able to access our e-learning content using both their desktop computer and their mobile device.

When developing our HTML5 project, we will also experience some of the current limitations of this technology. Although very powerful and promising, HTML5 is still fairly new and not yet able to reproduce all of the interactive and animated features that Flash has made us accustomed to. As Captivate developers, this means that some of the Captivate objects and effects cannot (yet?) be used in a mobile-friendly project.

In this chapter, we will:

- Capture onscreen action using one of the automatic recording modes
- Explore HTML5 compliant objects and features of Captivate 7
- Work with the mouse object
- Insert audio narration and video into a project
- Add click boxes and buttons to create interactivity
- Test the HTML5 output in a web browser

Fasten your seatbelts and let the mobile learning adventure begin!

Viewing the finished application

First, experience the finished application using an HTML5 compliant web browser. This testing situation is very close to the situation in which our students will experience our final content.

The HTML5 compliance of your browser

Go to `http://html5test.com/` to see the HTML5 compliance score of your browser and to see what is the most HTML5 compliant browser at the time of your reading.

1. Open the `finished/published/hdstreet/index.html` file of your exercises folder in an HTML5 compliant browser.
2. Click on the play icon at the center of the browser window.

At the time of this writing, the HTML5 output of Captivate can be played back on Internet Explorer 9 or later, Safari 5.1 or later, and Google Chrome 17 or later. If you try to view the application in another browser, the following message will pop up:

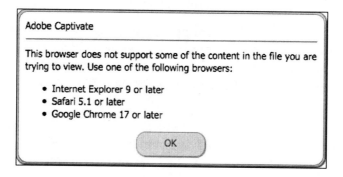

Download a browser for testing

If you do not have any one of the browsers listed in the previous screenshot, installed on your system, you can download Google Chrome for free at the URL `https://www.google.com/intl/en/chrome/browser/`.

While viewing this sample application, pay special attention to the interactivity features of this project. Once the introduction sequence is over, the project displays the site's home page and waits for the student to click on any one of the available links to view the corresponding sequence. This type of interactivity keeps the student involved, and at the center of the learning process.

During the rest of this chapter, we will go through the first two steps of the typical Captivate production workflow and reproduce this sample application. The Publishing step will be explained in detail in *Chapter 5, Publishing a Captivate Project for Mobile*.

The `finished/HDSB_finished.cptx` file in the exercises folder is the source file of the previous sample application. Refer to this file if something is unclear while doing the exercises of this chapter.

Capturing the slides

Capturing the slides is the first step of the typical Captivate production workflow. Unlike an HD Video Demo, that is recording using full-motion recording, a simulation is recorded using screen captures.

Preparing the application to capture

Our goal is to create an interactive virtual tour of the HD Street Band's website. Once again we will use our default web browser to view the band's website.

Open the `HDStreet-Site/index.html` file in your default web browser.

Your web browser is now ready for the capture session.

Rehearsing the scenario

The size of this project needs to match the size of an iPad screen in landscape mode (1024 x 672). The width of the HD Street Band's website has been calculated to fit in the 1024 pixels available on the iPad screen in landscape mode. But for the height of the site, the story is different. On the website, each page has a different height that depends on its content. The height of an iPad screen in landscape mode is 672 pixels, so a vertical scroll bar will appear on most (if not all) of the pages of our website when viewed on an iPad. This scroll bar, and all of the associated scroll bar actions, will need to be captured by Captivate, so it is important to mimic that situation when rehearsing the scenario.

1. Resize your browser window as shown in the following screenshot:

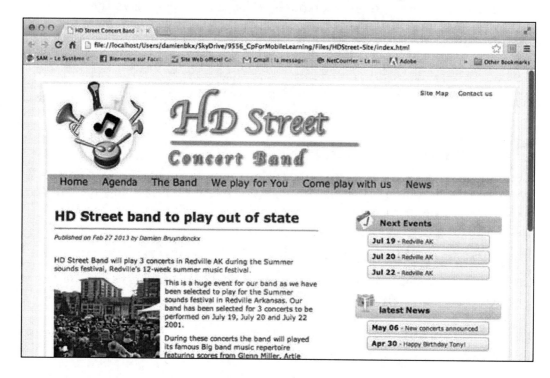

The scenario of this project is available in the book's sample files:

2. Open the `HDStreetVirualTour_scenario.pdf` file situated in your exercises folder.

3. Perform the steps described in the PDF file in your web browser.

Make sure you do not resize your browser window while rehearsing this scenario. Also, don't hesitate to go through the scenario as many times as needed until you master all of the steps in the correct order. Then, return to the site's home page and leave the browser open.

Getting Captivate ready for the capture session

Now that you've mastered the scenario, it is time to prepare Captivate for the capture session as shown in the following steps:

1. Open Adobe Captivate 7.
2. On the right-hand side of the welcome screen, click on the **Create New Software Simulation** link.

This is different than in the first chapter where we used the Video Demo link.

3. At the top of the recording window, choose to record an **Application**.
4. Open the **Select the window to record** drop-down menu, and choose your web browser in the list of opened applications.
5. In the **Snap To** section, choose the **Custom Size** option.
6. Open the **Custom** drop-down menu and choose the **Apple iPad landscape (1024 x 672)** preset.

The red recording area and your web browser's window both resize to the size of an iPad screen in landscape mode.

7. At the bottom of the recording window, make sure the recording mode is set to **Automatic**.
8. Select the **Demo** recoding mode and make sure that the other recording modes (**Assessment, Training,** and **Custom**) are deselected.
9. Leave the **Panning** option to **No Panning** and the **Audio** to **No Narration**.

Before moving on, make sure your recording window looks like the following screenshot:

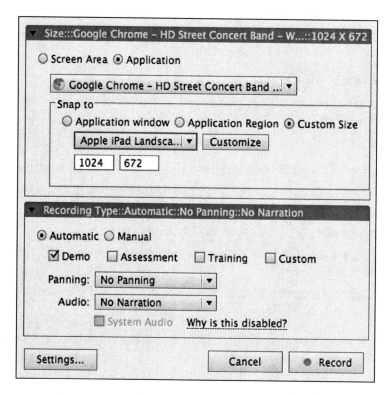

 A full discussion on the automatic recording modes of Captivate is beyond the scope of this book. For a more comprehensive guide, refer to the *Mastering Adobe Captivate 6* book by Packt Publishing at http://www.packtpub.com/mastering-adobe-captivate-6/book.

Reviewing Captivate preferences

One last thing to do before we start the actual capture session is to make sure that the preferences of Captivate are correctly adjusted. Perform the following steps:

1. Click on the **Settings** button situated at the bottom-left corner of the recording window.

After a short while, the **Preferences** window of Captivate opens on the **Recording | Modes** category.

2. Open the **Mode** drop-down menu.

3. Choose **Demonstration** from the **Mode** drop-down menu.

4. At the end of the **Preferences** window, click on the **Restore Default** link.

This action resets the **Demonstration** recording mode to default. Normally, three checkboxes should be selected:

- The **Add Text Captions** checkbox that instructs Captivate to generate text captions automatically during the capture

 If you want Captivate to generate a smart shape with text instead of text captions, select the **Use Smart Shapes instead of Captions** checkbox.

- The **Show Mouse Location and Movements** checkbox that instructs Captivate to automatically generate the mouse object

- The **Add Highlight Boxes on Click** checkbox that instructs Captivate to automatically generate a highlight box object each time a `Click` event occurs during the capture

Each of these automatically generated objects can be adjusted or even deleted during the editing step of the workflow.

5. In the left column of the **Preferences** window, click on the **Settings** category.

6. Notice the **Generate Captions In** drop-down menu. You can eventually change this preference to match your own language.

7. Make sure that the **Camera Sounds** checkbox is selected.

Thanks to this option, Captivate plays a camera shutter sound each time a screenshot is taken during the capture.

8. Make sure the **Smoothen movements for Drag and Drop actions** and **Mouse Wheel Actions** are both selected.

9. Leave all of the other options to their default settings, and click on the **OK** button to close the **Preferences** window.

Everything is now ready for the shooting session to begin.

Capture the onscreen action

We will now click on the **Record** button of Captivate and perform the actions described in the scenario. To ensure the success of the Capture phase, make sure you apply these simple tips and tricks:

- Perform the actions *slowly*.
- Turn your audio system on, so that you can hear the camera shutter sound each time Captivate generates a slide.
- Perform the scrolling actions *very* slowly
- If you are not sure whether or not Captivate has generated a screenshot, use the *Prnt Scrn* key (Windows) or the *command + F6* shortcut (Mac) to manually capture an extra screenshot.

When you feel ready, it is time to concentrate, take a deep breath and let the show begin!

1. Click on the **Record** button at the bottom-right corner of the recording window.

2. After the countdown, perform all of the actions described in the scenario.

3. When done, use the *End* key (Windows) or the *command + Enter* shortcut (Mac) to stop the recording.

Don't worry if you don't get it right on the first attempt. If you made a mistake, just end the recording, return to the home page of the site, and have another take!

Previewing the project

When you hit the *End* key (windows) or the *command + Enter* shortcut (Mac), Captivate generates the slides and opens the project for editing. Perform the following steps:

1. Navigate to the **File | Save** menu item to save the file in your exercises folder as HDSB_<YourName>_Raw.cptx.

Note that this project uses the .cptx file extension and not the .cpvc file extension we used in the first chapter. Actually, the .cptx extension is the standard file extension of Captivate, while the .cpvc extension is used by Video Demo projects only.

2. Use the preview icon to preview the entire project (or press *F4* on your keyboard). Alternatively, you can go to **File | Preview | Project**.

While previewing the project, you should notice that Captivate has generated many text captions (or smart shapes) automatically. This is due to the **Add Text Captions** checkbox that we selected in the **Demonstration** recording mode while in the **Preferences** window. Also notice the blue semi-transparent rectangles that appear next to each mouse click. These objects are the highlight boxes that Captivate has generated. This happened because, we selected the **Add Highlight Boxes on click** option in the **Preferences** window. Finally, notice how the mouse object moves and clicks automatically.

3. When the preview is finished, close the **Preview** window to return to the standard Captivate application.

Another look at the Captivate interface

When Captivate has finished generating the slides and loads the project, you'll have another look at the Captivate interface. What you are seeing now is the standard Captivate interface. What we used in the first chapter was a specialized version of Captivate used only by Video Demo projects.

The basic structure of the interface is the same, but there are more tools and panels available. At the center of the screen is the stage showing the currently selected slide. Panels and toolbars are placed around the stage. Of special interest are the **PROPERTIES** panel at the right-hand side of the screen, the **TIMELINE** and **Master Slide** panels at the bottom of the screen, and the **FILMSTRIP** panel at the left-hand side of the screen.

The **FILMSTRIP** panel shows the slides of the project in a way that is similar to what is used in presentation programs, such as Microsoft PowerPoint or Apple Keynote.

The inner working of the Captivate capture engine

A typical Captivate project, such as the one we are working on, is based on static screenshots captured in .bmp format. Each of these screenshots is represented as a slide in the **FILMSTRIP** panel. During the capture phase, Captivate generates one static screenshot (in other words, one slide) for each click event. When a click event occurs, Captivate also records the position of the mouse in addition to the .bmp static screenshot. At runtime, Captivate reproduces the mouse movement by creating a curved path between the recorded mouse positions. This has the following consequences:

- Since only static screenshots and mouse coordinates are recorded, the overall size of the project is very low.

- Captivate does not reproduce the actual path taken by the mouse during the capture, but recreates mouse movements at runtime using the coordinates of the recorded `click` events. This is very different from what happened in the first chapter when recording a video demo project.
- The timing of the resulting project does not match the timing of the actions performed during the capture (unless you select the **Action in Real Time** checkbox by going to **Recording | Settings** category in the **Preferences** window).

This capture system works fine in most situations. Some mouse actions, however, cannot be captured using static screenshots. These actions are the drag-and-drop and the scrolling actions. These actions need to be captured frame-by-frame. Because we selected the **Smoothen movements for Drag and Drop actions** and **Mouse Wheel Actions** checkboxes while in the **Preferences** window, Captivate has automatically switched to the frame-by-frame recording mode (also known as the full-motion recording) whenever a drag-and-drop or scrolling action was detected during the capture. The camera icon visible in the **FILMSTRIP** panel at the bottom-left corner of the slide thumbnail easily identifies the slides captured by the frame-by-frame recording mode. These slides are also known as Full Motion Recording (FMR) slides.

The Capture phase of the workflow is now finished. In the rest of this chapter, we will concentrate on the editing phase.

Editing the project for mobile output

Captivate proposes many objects that can be added on top of the slides. These objects help us create an actual e-learning experience out of the raw material provided by the capture phase. Unfortunately, some of these objects are not supported in the HTML5 output of Captivate. In this section of the book, we will explore some of the mobile-friendly objects and features of Captivate 7.

For the sake of clarity and to speed up things, we will use one of the sample files you downloaded from the Internet for the rest of this chapter:

1. Go to the **File | Open** menu item to open the `HDSB_raw.cptx` file of the exercises folder.

2. Go to the **File | Save As** menu item to save this file as `HDSB_<yourName>.cptx`.

3. Once done, use the preview icon to preview the entire project or go to the **File | Preview | Project** menu item.

Apart from the objects that have been added and synchronized for you, this sample project should be very similar to the one you recorded in the first part of this chapter.

Getting to know the work file

The project we will be working with contains 32 slides. These slides are visible in the **FILMSTRIP** panel situated on the left-hand side of the screen.

1. Use the vertical scroll bar of the **FILMSTRIP** panel to take a quick look at the slides contained in the project.

Notice that some slides are surrounded by a colored outline. This colored outline visually identifies groups of slides within the **FILMSTRIP** panel.

2. Use the **FILMSTRIP** panel to select slide **1**.

3. Still in the **FILMSTRIP** panel, click on the small arrow situated in the top-left corner of the slide **1** thumbnail.

This action collapses the group of slides named **Home** which slide **1** belongs to. You can use the same technique to collapse the other slide groups present in the **FILMSTRIP** panel.

4. Click one more time on the arrow situated in the top-left corner of the slide **1** thumbnail in the **FILMSTRIP** panel to expand the **Home** slide group.

5. Use the **FILMSTRIP** panel to select slide **5**.

6. At the top of the **PROPERTIES** panel write `mainMenu` in the **Name** field and validate it with the *Enter* key.

Grouping and naming slides has no impact on the published project. These are two nice features that make our lives as e-learning developers much easier in identifying slides and organizing content.

 Grouping and naming slides actually has some impact on the published project, as this information is used when a table of contents is inserted. Inserting an automatic table of contents in the project will not be discussed any further in this book.

Applying a theme to the project

Themes were a new feature of Captivate 6. A theme is a collection of the following three elements:

- **Styles**: This will define the default and alternative styling of the objects
- **Master slides**: These are used to define background, objects, and layouts common to many slides
- **Skin**: It is used to define the playback controls, the border, and the table of content of a project

We will now apply a theme to the project, and take a look at the styles and at the master slides it contains.

1. Return to the HDSB_<yourName>.cptx project.
2. Use the **FILMSTRIP** panel to go to slide **3**. It may be necessary to expand the home group to access slide **3**.

Slide **3** contains three arrows and three rounded rectangles.

3. Click on any of these six objects to select it.
4. Take a look at the **Style** drop-down menu on the topmost section of the **PPOPERTIES** panel. The style currently applied to the selected object should be the **[Default Smart Shape Style]**.
5. Open the **Style** drop-down menu to take a look at the three available styles.
6. Open the **Master Slide** panel situated at the bottom of the screen, next to the **TIMELINE** panel.
7. Take a look at the master slides available in the **Master Slide** panel.

These styles and master slides are defined in the default theme of Captivate that is currently applied to this project. We will now apply another theme to the project and take a second look at the available styles and master slides.

8. Make sure that slide **3** is selected in the **FILMSTRIP** panel.

9. Go to the **Themes | Apply a New Theme** menu item.

10. Apply the `Theme/HDSB_mobile.cptm` theme situated in the sample files of this book.

Notice the `.cptm` file extension used by the Captivate themes.

11. Take some time to read the Captivate message about style overrides, then click on **Yes** to apply the new theme to the project.

12. Return to the **Master Slide** panel and take a look at the available master slides. They should be different than before.

13. Select any of the six smart shapes (three arrows and three rounded rectangles) on slide **3**. In the topmost section of the **PROPERTIES** panel, open the **Styles** drop-down menu. There should now be four styles in the drop-down menu.

14. Apply the `HDSB_CaptionnedHB` style to the six smart shapes of slide **3**.

> In order to reset the formatting properties, it may be necessary to apply another style to the selected shape before reapplying the `HDSB_CaptionnedHB` style.

When done, all six shapes of slide **3** should have the same semi-transparent orange fill and the same orange stroke.

Extra credit

Use the same procedure to apply the `HDSB_CaptionnedHB` style to the remaining smart shapes of the project. Don't forget to save the file when done.

> **Creating custom themes**
>
> Creating custom themes is beyond the scope of this book. Information on this subject can be found on the official Captivate blog at the URL `http://blogs.adobe.com/captivate/2012/06/how-to-create-custom-themes-in-adobe-captivate-6.html`.

Creating the introduction and ending slides

We will now use the available styles and master slides to add new content to this project. In this particular section, we will create a nice introduction slide at the beginning of the project as shown in the following steps:

1. Use the **FILMSTRIP** panel to select the first slide of the project.

2. Go to the **Insert | New slide from | Title Slide** menu item to insert a new slide based on the **Title Slide** master slide.

3. In the **FILMSTRIP** panel, drag the newly inserted slide up to make it the first slide of the project.

The new slide already contains a nice background image featuring the band's logo and a Text Caption placeholder on top of that background picture. These elements are defined on the **Title Slide** master slide. Also notice that our new slide is part of the home slide group.

4. Triple-click into the text caption placeholder to select the temporary text.

5. Type **HD Street Band's website** in the text caption.

6. Press the *Esc* key of your keyboard to select the text caption as an object.

With the new text caption selected, take a look at the topmost section of the **PROPERTIES** panel. Notice that the style currently applied to the text caption is the **HDSB-Title** style.

7. Click on an empty area of the slide to deselect the text caption.

The **PROPERTIES** panel now shows the properties of the slide. In the **General** section of the **PROPERTIES** panel notice that the **Title Slide** master slide is applied to slide **1**. Both the **Title Slide** master slide and the **HDSB-Title** style are defined in the HDSB_mobile theme we applied to the project earlier in this chapter.

Extra credit

Use the same techniques to insert a nice ending slide (based on the same **Title** master slide) at the very end of the project. Change the text of the placeholder text caption to **Thank you for watching this video**. Also, resize the text caption so the text nicely fits in the object. Don't forget to save the file when done. Your project should now contain 34 slides.

Using effects and transitions in a mobile-friendly project

Since the early days of Captivate 1, it has been possible to apply basic Fade In and/or Fade Out transitions to any objects. These simple transitions are perfectly supported in HTML5 and can be used with no restrictions in a mobile-friendly project, as shown in the following steps:

1. Use **FILMSTRIP** to return to the first slide of the project.
2. Select the text caption that reads **HD Street Band's website**.
3. In the **Transition** section of the **PROPERTIES** panel, open the **Effect** drop-down menu.
4. Apply the **Fade In Only** transition to the selected text caption.

We will now use **TIMELINE** to synchronize the text caption's Fade In transition with the slide.

5. Open the **TIMELINE** panel at the bottom of the screen.

The **TIMELINE** panel of slide 1 should contain two layers. The bottom layer represents the slide itself while the top layer contains the text caption.

6. Use your mouse to extend the display time of slide from 1 to 4 seconds.
7. Make the text caption appear after 1 second and display for the rest of the slide.

When done, the Timeline of slide 1 should be similar to the following image.

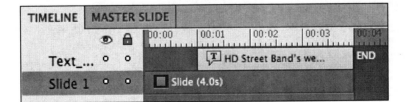

The strange red triangle

While moving objects on the **TIMELINE** panel, a red triangle might appear on some objects that are at the end of the **TIMELINE** panel. Read the great blog post by Kevin Siegel to know more about this red triangle at `http://iconlogic.blogs.com/weblog/2013/07/adobe-captivate-anchors-away.html`.

8. Use the **FILMSTRIP** panel to select the last slide of the project.

9. Repeat steps 3 to 7 to apply the same transition and timing on slide 34 to the text caption that reads **Thanks you for viewing this video**.

Don't forget to save the file.

Using the effects panel in a mobile-friendly project

In this section, we will apply a more sophisticated effect to the arrow smart shapes of slide 4. Of course, we will make sure that the applied effect is HTML5 compliant so that it can be played back on mobile devices.

1. Use the **FILMSTRIP** panel to go to slide 4, and click on the stage to select the topmost orange arrow.

The objects of this slide are already adjusted on the **TIMELINE** panel. For instance, the selected arrow appears at six seconds into the slide, is on display for six seconds and then disappears at 12 seconds into the slide.

Captivate proposes an entire array of effects in addition to the simple Fade In and Fade Out transitions we used in the previous section.

2. Go to the **Window | Effects** menu item to turn the **EFFECTS** panel on.

By default, the **EFFECTS** panel appears next to the **TIMELINE** and **MASTER SLIDE** panels at the bottom of the screen.

3. With the topmost arrow still selected, click on the **Add Effect** button situated at the bottom-left corner of the **EFFECTS** panel.

Take some time to inspect the available effects and to get used to the way they are categorized. These effects are similar to what is found in presentation programs, such as Microsoft PowerPoint and Apple Keynote.

All of these effects are fully supported by the Flash player, and can be used with no restrictions in projects that are to be published in .swf format. But in mobile-friendly projects published in HTML5, only a small subset of these effects is supported.

When it comes to HTML5 compliance, each effect falls under one of the following three categories:

- Some effects are not at all supported in HTML5. In Captivate 7, these effects are identified by a small star (*) by their names.

- A double star (**) identifies the effects that are partially supported in HTML5. These effects will look different in the HTML5 output than in the Flash (.swf) output.

- The remaining effects are fully supported in both the HTML5 and Flash output. They can be used with no restrictions at all.

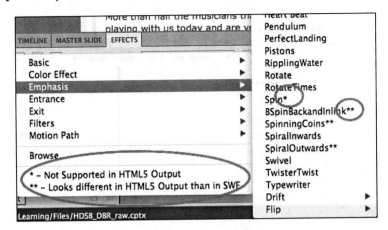

Using an unsupported effect does not prevent the project from getting published in HTML5, but the effect will be ignored and won't play in the HTML5 output.

4. Navigate to **Entrance | Fly in | Fly In From Left**, and apply this effect to the topmost arrow. Note that this effect has no star (*) or double star (**) behind it, so it is safe to use it in a mobile-friendly project.

5. In the **EFFECTS** panel, reduce the duration of the effect to the first second of the object's timeline.

 The duration of an effect is relative to the duration of the object the effect is applied to. In other words, if you change the duration of the object on the main Timeline, you also change the absolute duration of the effect.

6. Make sure that the **EFFECTS** panel of the topmost arrow is similar to the following screenshot:

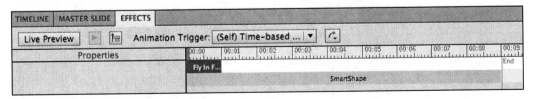

7. Repeat the above steps to apply the same **Fly In From Left** effect to the other two arrows of this slide.

8. Save the file when done.

Inserting multimedia components

One of the most significant new features of HTML5 is the ability to play multimedia content in the browser without the help of any third-party plugin. This is excellent news for us as we can take advantage of this new capability to add audio and video components to our mobile-friendly Captivate projects.

Inserting video files

Video can be inserted in both Flash and HTML5 projects. When publishing the project an external application called the **Adobe Media Encoder (AME)** automatically converts the video to the proper format if needed. The Adobe media encoder is part of the Captivate package.

In the next exercise, we will insert a new slide in the project and add a video clip onto it:

1. Use the **FILMSTRIP** panel to go to slide 1.
2. Navigate to the **Insert | New Slide From | Video Slide** menu item to insert a new slide into the project.

The new slide contains two placeholder objects on top of an image background.

3. Double-click the rounded rectangle placeholder in the upper area of the slide so that a blinking cursor appears in the middle of the rounded rectangle.
4. Write **Welcome!** in the rounded rectangle. Then, press the *Esc* key to exit the text edit mode and select the smart shape object.

The ability to write text into smart shapes is one of the reasons I consider smart shapes to be one of the best features of Captivate.

5. Double-click into the red text caption placeholder at the bottom of the slide.
6. Replace the placeholder text with `http://www.hdstreet.com`.
7. Your new slide should now look like the following screenshot:

8. Go to the **Video | Insert Video** menu item to open the **Insert Video** dialog.

9. At the top of the dialog, make sure that the **Multi-Slide Synchronized Video** option is selected.

10. Click on the **Browse** button and insert the `Video/slide2.mp4` file situated in the sample files of this book.

Captivate is able to insert video files with the extensions `.flv`, `.f4v`, `.avi`, `.mp4`, `.mov`, and `.3gp`.

11. Make sure the **Video Type** is set to **Progressive download**; as video streaming is not supported in HTML5.

12. At the end of the **Insert Video** dialog, select the **Modify slide duration to accommodate video** option.

13. Leave all of the other options at their default settings and click on the **OK** button.

The video file should appear in the middle of slide 2 between the smart shape and the text caption.

14. Open the **TIMELINE** panel at the bottom of the screen.

There should be four layers in **TIMELINE** of slide 2. The bottom layer represents the slide itself. The other three layers represent the three objects placed on this slide. You will now arrange these objects on the **TIMELINE** panel.

15. In the **TIMELINE** panel, move the **Video** layer (the topmost layer) to the right, so that the video begins half a second into the slide.

16. Move to the end of the **TIMELINE** panel and extend the display time of the slide (the bottom layer) to 42 seconds.

17. Make the **Welcome** smart shape display for the entire duration of the slide (42 seconds).

18. Make the Text Caption with the site URL appear at 35.5 seconds into the slide and display to the end of the slide.

 The labels in the left column of **TIMELINE**, as seen on the following screenshot, have been modified to help you understand the screenshot. It is normal if they are different than your computer screen.

The **TIMELINE** panel of **Slide 2** should be similar to the following screenshot:

Adding audio narration

In a typical Captivate project, audio clips (with extensions: .wav or .mp3) can be added at three different levels:

- **Object level**: The sound associated with an object plays when the object appears on the screen. This is a great place to add small sound effects (whoosh, clings, bangs, tones, and so on) to the project.

- **Slide level**: The audio clip plays in sync with the slide. Most of the time, this option is used to add voice-over narration.

- **Project level**: The audio clip is used to add background music to the entire project.

All of these options are supported in HTML5. However, you should avoid *overlapping* audio in a mobile-friendly project.

 This overlapping audio issue is explained in great details in the help article at http://helpx.adobe.com/captivate/using/ publish-projects-html5-files.html#main-pars_heading_4.

To avoid overlapping audio in this project, you'll only use audio at the slide level. You will also use the **LIBRARY** panel to insert the audio clips in the project as shown in the following steps:

1. Open the **LIBRARY** panel situated next to the **PROPERTIES** panel.
2. At the top of the **LIBRARY** panel, click on the import icon.
3. Go to the **Audio** folder of the exercise files and select all the .wav files it contains. Import them into the project's library.

Captivate imports the selected audio files one-by-one. When completed, you should have 23 audio files in the **Audio** folder of the library named after the slide they will be inserted on.

4. Open the **FILMSTRIP** panel and select **Slide 3**.
5. Drag the slide03.wav audio file from the **Audio** section of the **LIBRARY** panel, and drop it on top of **Slide 3**. Make sure you don't drop it on an object of the slide, otherwise the audio will be imported onto the object not onto the slide.

6. In the **Audio Import Options** dialog, select the **Show the slide for the same amount of time as the length of the audio file** option.

Take a look at the **TIMELINE** panel. The audio waveform appears in its own layer below the slide layer.

7. In the **TIMELINE** panel, move the audio waveform so the narration begins half a second into the slide.

8. Repeat the above actions for the remaining 22 audio files.

9. Don't forget to save the file after moving all the audio files onto the slides.

Working with the mouse

The mouse object is what makes the mouse visible to the learner in the final project. This object has been automatically generated by the demonstration recording mode we used to capture the slides of this project.

1. Go to the **FILMSTRIP** panel to select slide 7.

2. Go to the **Modify | Mouse | Show Mouse** menu item to hide the mouse object from this slide. Alternatively, you can click on the mouse icon situated in the **FILMSTRIP** panel next to slide 7 to access the same option.

Hiding the mouse does not remove it from the slide; should you change your mind about the mouse being hidden.

3. Use **FILMSTRIP** to go to slide 10. It may be necessary to expand the **Agenda** slide group to access slide 10.

4. Click on the mouse cursor to select the mouse object, and open the **PROPERTIES** panel if needed.

As expected, the **PROPERTIES** panel shows the properties of the **Mouse** object. Take some time to review these properties. Most of them should be self-explanatory. All these properties can be used in a mobile-friendly project except for two little details.

- The **Show Mouse Click** option can only use the default mouse click animation in a mobile-friendly project.

- If you select the **Mouse Click Sound** option, use the TIMELINE panel to make sure that the `Click` event does not occur when another audio track is playing in order to avoid the overlapping audio problem mentioned earlier.

The **Mouse** object also appears in the **TIMELINE** panel. This means that the mouse can be synchronized with the rest of the slide using the same techniques as with the other objects in Captivate as shown in following steps:

1. Use the **FILMSTRIP** panel to select slide 3. It may be necessary to expand the **Home** slide group to access slide 3.

With slide 3 selected, take a look at the **TIMELINE** panel. It should contain three layers. The topmost layer is the mouse object.

2. Use your mouse to move the **Mouse** object to the end of the **TIMELINE** panel so that its position matches the following screenshot:

Adding interactivity with buttons and click boxes

Captivate offers three interactive objects that are all supported in HTML5. These objects have the unique ability to stop the playhead and wait for the student to do something. In this exercise we will use buttons and click boxes.

Working with buttons

The first interactive object is the Button object that we will add on slide 2 as shown in the following steps:

1. Use the **FILMSTRIP** panel to select slide 2.

2. Go to the **Insert | Standard Objects | Button** menu item or the **Insert** Button icon to create a new button.

3. Move the button to the bottom-right corner of the slide on top of the bottom yellow stripe.

Captivate 7 will display a dotted green line when the button is aligned with the copyright notice situated in the bottom-left corner. This dotted line is known as a Smart Guide. Use it to easily align objects together. Smart Guides is a new feature of Captivate 7.

4. In the **Action** section of the **PROPERTIES** panel make sure that the **On Success** action of the button is set to **Go to the next slide**.

5. Also make sure that the **Infinite Attempts** checkbox is selected.

6. Under **Timing**, make sure that the pause is set for 1.5 seconds.

7. Move the button to the very end of the **TIMELINE** panel.

With these settings, our button simply stops the playhead and waits for the click of the student to jump to the next slide, and continue with the course.

Extra credit

Go to slide 7 and insert a second button. Place this button at the end of the main navigation bar next to the **News** link. Use the **PROPERTIES** panel to apply the **HDSB-ButtonDone** style to this button. In the **Action** section of the **PROPERTIES** panel, set the **On Success action** to **Jump To Slide 35**. Finally, move the button to the end of the **TIMELINE** panel. Make sure this second button looks like the following screenshot:

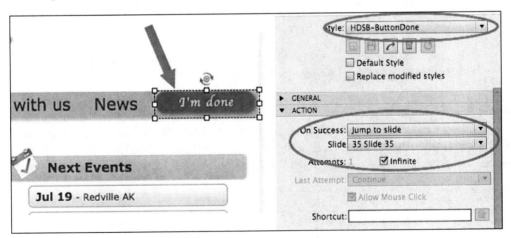

Working with click boxes

The second interactive object we will be working with is the click box object. A click box is a transparent rectangle that defines a sensitive area on the slide. The click box is able to trigger an action when the student clicks inside of this sensitive area, and (optionally) another action when the student clicks outside of the sensitive area. Perform the following steps:

1. Use the **FILMSTRIP** panel to select slide 7.

2. Navigate to the **Insert | Standard Objects | Click Box** menu item or click on the insert click box icon to create a new click box object.

3. Move and resize the new click box to place it on top of the **Home** button of the main navigation bar of the site.

 When positioning the click box on top of the **Home** button, keep in mind that on a mobile device, students will use their finger to tap on the click box instead of their mouse to click on it. Don't hesitate to make the click box a bit bigger that what's actually needed in order to offer the finger a large enough tap target.

4. In the **Options** section of the **PROPERTIES** panel, make sure the **Success, Failure,** and **Hint** Captions checkboxes are deselected.

5. In the **Action** section of the **PROPERTIES** panel, set the **On Success** action to **Jump to slide 3 homeDebut** and leave the **Infinite** checkbox selected.

Notice how the slide name comes in handy when setting up the action of the click box.

6. In the **Timing** section of the **PROPERTIES** panel, make the click box **Appear After 0 sec** and **Display For** the **Rest of the Slide.**

Extra credit

Insert 7 more click boxes on this slide. Refer to the following table for the location and the action of these click boxes. The other properties of these click boxes are the same as the properties we applied on the first click box we inserted together.

	Location	Action
1	On top of the **Agenda** link	Jump to slide 8 – agendaDebut
2	On top of the **The Band** link	Jump to slide 13 – bandDebut
3	On top of the **We play for you** link	Jump to slide 18 – wePlayForYouDebut
4	On top of the **Come play with us** link	Jump to slide 23 – comePlayDebut
5	On top of the **News** link	Jump to slide 28 – NewsDebut

	Location	Action
6	On top of the **Site Map** link	Jump to slide 33 – Site Map
7	On top of the **Contact Us** link	Jump to slide 34 – Contact Us

Finalizing interactivity

The click boxes we added in the previous sections allow the students to choose the order in which they want to view the different sequences of the video. To finalize this process, we will now instruct Captivate to return to slide 7 at the end of each sequence:

1. Use the **FILMSTRIP** panel to go to slide 12 (slide 12 is the last slide of the **Agenda** sequence).

2. In the **Action** section of the **PROPERTIES** panel, set the **On Exit** action of slide 12 to **Jump to slide 7 mainMenu**.

3. Repeat step 2 on slides 17, 22, 27, 32, 33, and 34.

 You can also select slides 12, 17, 22, 27, 32, 33, and 34 in the **FILMSTRIP** panel using your mouse and the *command* (Mac) or *Ctrl* (Windows) key, and apply the same **On Exit** action to all the selected slides at once.

Don't forget to test your actions and then save the file.

Previewing the HTML5 output

Our project should now be ready for previewing. To make sure that every single detail has been taken care of, we will now test the HTML5 output of our project in a compliant web browser as follows:

1. Navigate to the **File | Preview | HTML5 Output In Web Browser** menu item to create a temporary version of the HTML5 project and play it in the default browser.

Captivate generates the slides of the project and plays the project in the default web browser.

2. Preview the entire project in your web browser as if you were a student. Make sure everything works as expected. If something is not functioning correctly, return to Captivate to address the problem.

3. When everything is exactly the way you want it, save and close the project.

In *Chapter 5, Publishing a Captivate Project for Mobile*, we will cover the publishing step of this project in great detail.

Summary

In this chapter, you created a Captivate simulation using the demonstration mode, and ensured it is mobile-friendly. To do so, you went through the first two steps of the typical Captivate production workflow:

- In the first step, the capture step, you created the project using one of the iPad presets of Captivate
- In the second step, the editing step, you used the standard Captivate interface to slowly transform your project into interactive e-learning content

Along the way, you discovered some of the objects and features available in Captivate 7.

You discovered that many of these objects and features are not fully supported in a mobile-friendly project. On the other end, other objects and features are perfectly supported in HTML5 and can be used with no restriction in any Captivate projects.

Finally, you tested the HTML5 output of your project in a compliant web browser in order to ensure that all components work as expected.

In the next chapter, you will start from an existing project that has been created for the Flash player, and you will learn how to convert it into a mobile-friendly project.

3

Optimizing an Existing
Project for Mobile

So far in this book, we have created new projects that we knew would be viewed on mobile devices. When creating these first two projects, we could therefore ensure that we were only using the mobile-friendly features and objects of Captivate 7.

In this chapter, we will start from an existing project developed with the Flash player in mind. When this project was created, the Flash platform was the dominant technology for building the interactive and animated content that Captivate enables us to author. But today, due to the widespread success of mobile devices, many companies are converting their existing projects to HTML5.

We will first take a look at the Flash project and identify the unsupported objects. We will then go through each of these unsupported objects, one-by-one, and see how we can replace them with things that are supported in HTML5. Along the way, we will uncover some more features of Captivate 7, including the **HTML5 Tracker**, the **Slide Notes** panel, the **text-to-speech** engine, the **rollover objects**, the **text animations**, **object grouping**, and even simple advanced actions.

At the end of this chapter, our existing project will be ready to be published for mobile devices with HTML5.

Viewing the sample project

First, take a look at the original project by performing the following steps:

1. Open the `drivingInBe_start.cptx` file.
2. Navigate to **File | Save As** to save this file as `drivingInBe_mobile.cptx`.

3. Use the preview icon to preview the entire project. Alternatively, you can go to the **File | Preview | Project** menu item or the *F4* shortcut key.

 Creating this project is discussed in great details in *Mastering Adobe Captivate 6* by Packt Publishing. See http://www.packtpub.com/ mastering-adobe-captivate-6/book for details.

This Preview mode uses Flash technology, so every single feature of Captivate is fully supported. While previewing this project, pay special attention to the following:

- The animated text on the first and last slide
- The rollover objects on slides 13, 14, and 15

When the project is finished, close the **Preview** window. Don't hesitate to preview this project a few more times. Give different answers to the questions asked on slides 5 and 9 at each preview. Notice that the feedback messages you get depend on the answers you give. The ability to react differently based on the student's actions and answers is known as **Branching**.

Before we move on, let's make one last experiment:

4. Use the preview icon to preview the **HTML5 Output In Web Browser**. Alternatively, you can go to the **File | Preview | HTML5 Output In Web Browser** menu item.

Pay close attention to the message that pops up, as shown in the following screenshot:

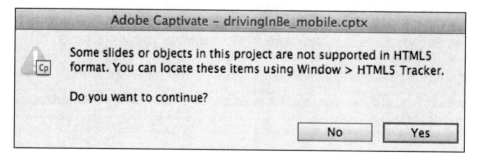

5. Click on **Yes** to continue with the preview.
6. When the project has finished loading in the browser, click on the play icon at the center of the first slide.

Watch the entire project as it plays in the browser and pay close attention to the following:

- The text animations on the first and last slides have been replaced by static text
- The button on slide 3 does not show and the movie does not pause
- The rollover objects of slides 13, 14, and 15 are not working

 If you are using Captivate 6 or 6.1, the list of unsupported features is a bit longer, as support for some of the effects used in this file have been added in Captivate 7.

The HTML5 Tracker

The **HTML5 Tracker** is a panel that makes it easy to identify the objects and features of a project that are not supported in HTML5.

1. Still in the `drivingInBe_mobile.cptx` project, go to the **Window | HTML5 Tracker** menu item to open the **HTML5 Tracker** panel.

The **HTML5 Tracker** panel opens and displays a list of unsupported objects.

Some of the unsupported features we have noticed while testing the HTML5 output in the browser are not listed in the **HTML5 Tracker**. As a best practice, we should therefore always test the HTML5 output in a web browser, even if the **HTML5 Tracker** displays an empty list.

Dealing with unsupported features

In this section, we will review each of the unsupported features of the project. We will discuss various ways to deal with these unsupported features in order to provide a nice user experience on mobile devices. Let's start by looking at the elements listed in the **HTML5 Tracker** panel.

Text animations

The first unsupported item listed in the **HTML5 Tracker** is the text animation object situated on slide 1. There are two different approaches to address this issue:

- First, we can decide to leave things the way they are. The text animation object provides a nice looking effect for the students using the Flash version of the content. On mobile devices, this text animation gracefully degrades into a static text caption, which is perfectly acceptable in many situations. If you choose to use this approach, you must accept that the user experience on a desktop computer will be slightly different than the user experience on a mobile device.

- The second approach is to delete the text animation and to replace it with an object that is supported in HTML5 (in this case, a standard text caption or a smart shape). The main advantage of this approach is that each student has the same user experience while viewing the content. We can also apply basic effects to the text caption (using the **Transition** section of the **PROPERTIES** panel or the **EFFECTS** panel) that will play the same way on both desktop and mobile devices.

For this exercise, you will use the second approach and replace the text animation with a standard text caption.

 The finished mobile version of the project is available in the exercise files as /finished/drivingInBe_mobile.cptx. Use it as reference when doing the exercises of this chapter.

1. Use the **FILMSTRIP** panel to select the first slide of the project.
2. Select the text animation that reads **Driving in Belgium**.
3. Take some time to inspect the position of this object on the **TIMELINE** panel.

Note that this object appears at one second into the slide and stays on display during four seconds until the end of the slide.

4. Delete the text animation object, then the text animation placeholder.
5. Go to the **Insert | Standard Object | Text Caption** menu item, or the insert text caption icon of the vertical toolbar, to insert a new text caption on slide 1.
6. Replace the default text by **Driving In Belgium**.
7. Press the *Esc* key to exit the text edit mode and leave the text caption object selected.
8. In the topmost area of the **PROPERTIES** panel, apply the **MFTC-Title** style to the new text caption.
9. Resize the text caption so the text fits comfortably in the object. Then move the object to place it roughly where the text animation used to be.
10. Arrange the **TIMELINE** panel so that the new text caption appears at one second into the slide and displays for four seconds until the end of the slide.
11. In the **Transition** section of the **PROPERTIES** panel, change the **Effect** to **Fade In Only**.

Extra credit

Repeat the previous procedure with the text animation situated on the last slide of the project.

Rollover objects

Captivate offers three types of rollover objects. The rollover objects allow you to add cool interactivity to your project. These objects are originally hidden from the slide and are revealed when the student hovers over a sensitive area (called a **Rollover Area**) with the mouse. The problem is that mobile devices are touch devices. The student uses their finger to interact with the application, not their mouse. This makes rollover objects impossible to use on a mobile device. These objects are, therefore, not supported in the HTML5 output of Captivate.

Rollover slidelet

The first rollover object we will focus on is the **rollover slidelet**. In our project, the rollover slidelet is showcased on slide 13.

1. Use the **FILMSTRIP** panel to go to slide 13 of the `drivingInBe_mobile.cptx` project.
2. Click on the brownish rectangle that covers the center of the screen.

The brownish rectangle that you just selected is the rollover slidelet. Notice that a blue border appears on top of the **Convert speeds to MPH** text caption situated in the top-right corner of the slide. This blue border marks the rollover area that is associated with the rollover slidelet. The brownish rectangle is originally hidden from the slide and appears only when the student hovers over the rollover area.

3. Use the preview icon to preview the project **From This Slide**. Alternatively, you can go to the **File | Preview | From This Slide** menu item, or the use *F8* (Windows) or *command + F8* (Mac) shortcut key.

In the **Preview** window, notice that the rollover slidelet is not displayed when the slide first appears.

4. Roll your mouse over the **Convert Speeds to MPH** text caption. The rollover slidelet appears and plays its own Timeline.
5. Close the **Preview** Window.

At the time of this writing, it is not possible to reproduce the exact same interaction in HTML5. While addressing this issue, we will therefore keep the following two things in mind:

- Because `Rollover` events are not supported on mobile devices, we must use standard `Click` events (or `Tap` events on mobile devices) to show and hide objects.
- The most important thing is to make the content of the rollover slidelet (the three text captions) available to students using mobile devices.

This situation illustrates the fact that, due to the constraints of mobile devices, the content is the most important thing to focus on when developing mobile e-learning.

 If you want information on this topic, I strongly recommend the book *Mobile First* by Luke Wroblewsky in the *A book apart* collection, which can be found at http://www.abookapart.com/products/mobile-first.

We will now delete the rollover slidelet and replace it with standard objects. We will use click boxes and advanced actions to recreate the interactivity.

6. Still on slide 13, select the rollover slidelet and delete it.

Note that deleting the rollover slidelet also deletes the associated rollover area.

7. Open the `helpers/DIB_Slide13.cptx` file situated in the exercises.

8. Select all of the objects situated on the first (and only) slide of this project. There should be six objects in the selection.

9. Copy and paste the selected objects on slide 13 of the `drivingInBe_mobile.cptx` project.

We will use these six objects (a rounded rectangle, three text captions, a close button, and a click box) to replace the rollover slidelet that we just deleted.

Grouping objects

The ability to group objects together is a very handy feature of Captivate.

1. Make sure all six of the objects you just pasted are selected. If not, select them now.

2. Go to the **Edit | Group** menu item to group the selected objects together. Alternatively, you can use a right-click, or the *Ctrl + g* (Windows) or *command + g* (Mac) shortcut to perform the same operation.

With the group selected, the **PROPERTIES** panel should show the properties pertaining to the entire group.

3. At the top of the **PROPERTIES** panel change the name of the group to `grp_convertMph`.

4. In the leftmost area of the **TIMELINE** panel, click on the arrow next to the group's name to expand the group content. Click a second time on the same arrow to collapse the group.

This group will be a huge time saver when developing the slidelet-like interaction later in this chapter.

Creating the initial state of the interaction

Remember that the rollover slidelet is initially hidden from the slide. To reproduce this situation, turn the visibility of the `grp_convertMph` group off.

1. Make sure the `grp_convertMph` group is still selected.

2. In the topmost section of the **PROPERTIES** panel, deselect the **Visible in Output** checkbox.

This action makes the group invisible in the published version of the project, but not in the editing environment of Captivate.

3. In the leftmost section of the **TIMELINE** panel, turn the visibility of the group off as shown in the following screenshot:

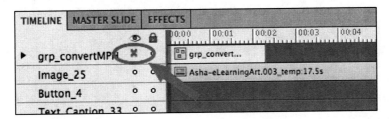

This action makes the group invisible in the editing environment of Captivate, but not in the published version.

To see or not to see

The two features that we just used induce lots of confusion to many Captivate users. The difference between the eye icon of **TIMELINE** panel and the **Turn Off Visibility** checkbox of the **PROPERTIES** panel is that the former only turns the visibility off in the editing environment, but not in the published project. The latter makes the object invisible in the published project, but not in the editing environment. Note that in our case, deselecting the **Turn Off Visibility** checkbox is the only required thing. But for a distracted person like me, having the editing environment match the published project is a must, so I also use the eye icon of the **TIMELINE** panel!

Create an advanced action to show the group

In this section, we will create an **Advanced Action** that will be used to turn the visibility of the group On:

1. Go to the **Project | Advanced Actions** menu item to open the **Advanced Actions** dialog box.

2. Type showConvertGroup in the **Action Name** field.

3. Double-click in the first row of the **Advanced Actions** and choose **Show** in the list of actions.

4. In the second drop-down menu, choose **grp_convertMPH**. Make sure the **Advanced Actions** dialog looks like the following screenshot:

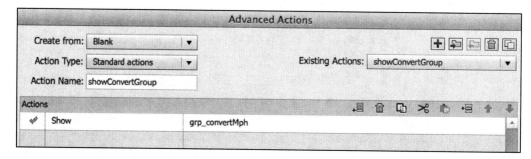

5. Click on the **Save As Action** button situated at the bottom-right corner of the **Advanced Actions** dialog, acknowledge the successful save of the action and close the **Advanced Actions** dialog.

Now that the advanced action is created, we must bind it to a Click (or a Tap) event.

Binding advanced actions to events

Binding an action to an event is deciding when an action is triggered. In our case, we want the advanced action to be triggered when the student clicks (or taps) the **Convert Speeds to MPH** text caption.

See the wonderful post by Lieve Weymeis for more on actions and events in Captivate at http://blog.lilybiri.com/events-and-advanced-actions.

To do so, we will use a click box to define the sensitive area of the Click (or Tap) event, and we will bind our action to the On Success event of the click box.

1. Go to **Insert | Standard Objects | Click Box** or the insert click box icon in the vertical toolbar to insert a new click box.

2. Move and resize the click box so it roughly covers the **Convert Speeds to MPH** text caption.

 Don't hesitate to make the click box a bit larger than what is needed to give the student's finger a large enough tap target.

3. In the **Options** section of the **PROPERTIES** panel, make sure the **Success**, **Failure**, and **Hint** captions are all deselected.

4. Also deselect the **Pause project until user clicks** option. Pausing the project is handled by the **Continue** Button.

5. In the **Action** section of the **PROPERTIES** panel, open the **On Success** drop-down menu and choose **Execute Advanced Actions**.

6. In the **script** drop-down menu that appears directly below, choose the **showConvertGroup** action.

7. Finally, move the click box and the **grp_convertMPH** group to the very end of the **TIMELINE** panel.

 It is necessary to turn the visibility of the group back on the **TIMELINE** panel to be able to move it to the end of the **TIMELINE** panel.

8. Go to **File | Preview | From This Slide** menu item to test the new interaction. Make sure everything functions as expected before moving onto the next exercise.

Notice also how grouping objects have helped you creating the advanced action!

Extra credit – create the hide action

The last thing to do is to create another advanced action to hide the group. This action needs to be triggered when clicking (or tapping) on the click box that is included in the **grp_convertMPH** group. General steps are as follow:

1. In the **TIMELINE** panel, turn the visibility of the group back on.

2. Navigate to the **Project | Advanced Actions** menu item to create the hideGrpConvert action.

3. Assign the new action to the On Success event of the click box that is inside the group.

After you complete this, use preview to test both the Show and the Hide functions of the interaction. Don't forget to save the file before moving on to the next section.

Rollover caption

The second rollover object that we need to convert to be mobile-friendly is the rollover caption object that is showcased on slide 14 of the `drivingInBe_mobile.cptx` project. Perform the following steps:

1. Use the **FILMSTRIP** panel to go to slide 14 of the project.
2. Select any of the three brownish text captions in the middle of the slide.

Notice that when selecting a rollover text caption, a corresponding rollover area is highlighted in a blue stroke.

3. Go to the **File | Preview | From This Slide** menu item to experiment with the rollover caption object.
4. Close the **Preview** window when done.

 The rollover objects on this slide are actually rollover smart shapes. Rollover smart shapes and rollover captions differ only by the actual shape of the object, but their interactive behavior is the same.

While we could use the same approach to what we did for the rollover slidelet object, we will explore another feature of Captivate instead. We will now delete the rollover smart shapes from the slide and replace them by an **advanced learning interaction**.

5. Select all three rollover smart shapes and delete them. This also deletes their corresponding rollover areas.
6. Also delete the other objects present on the slide, except for the **Continue** button. Make sure the **Continue** button is the only object left on the slide before moving on.

Advanced learning interactions have been developed with both the Flash and the HTML5 output in mind. Meaning that these objects can be used in Captivate projects published for desktop computers and mobile devices.

7. Navigate to the **Insert | Interactions** menu item to open the **Select Interaction** dialog box.

The list of available interactions depends on the exact update patch applied to your Captivate installation.

8. Click on the **Tabs** interaction to select it (shown in the following screenshot).

9. Click on the **Insert** button at the bottom-right corner of the **Select Interaction** dialog.

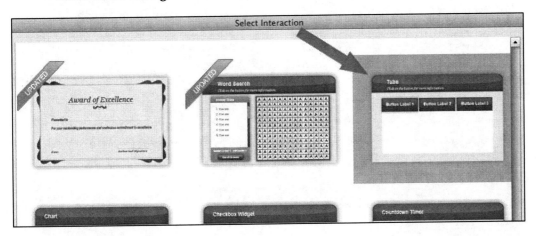

The smart learning interactions of Captivate are configurable static widgets. We will now us the **Configure interaction** dialog to customize the tab widget.

10. In the left column of the **Configure interaction** dialog, choose the most appropriate **theme** (in the sample files, we used theme 15).

By default, the **Tabs** interaction comes with 4 tabs on the Mac and 3 tabs on Windows. In our exercise, we only need three tabs.

11. In the main area, double-click on **Button label 4**. This step is only for the Mac users.

12. Click on the minus icon that appears in order to delete the fourth button. This step is only for the Mac users.

13. In the header area, double-click on the **Title** placeholder text and change it to **Parking In Belgium**. Also change the **Description** placeholder text to **Review those Belgian road signs about parking**.

14. Double-click on the **Button Label 1** and change the text to **No Parking anytime**.

15. Double-click on the **Button Content 1** area.

16. Click on the **Add Image** icon situated on the left-hand side of the **Button Content 1** area.

17. In the **Select Image from Library** dialog, select the e3_noParking.png image and click on the **OK** button.

18. Double-click on the **Insert button content here** placeholder text and type **This road sign means that no parking is allowed at any time in this area!**

The first tab of the interaction should now look like the following screenshot:

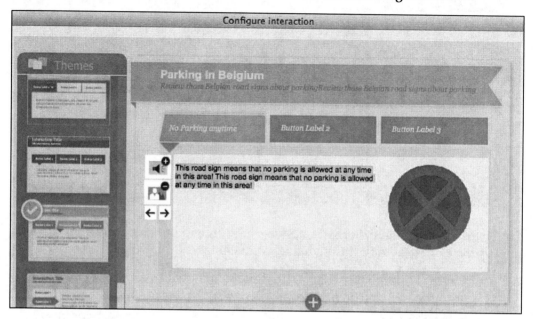

19. Repeat steps 13 to 16 with the remaining two tabs. Refer to the following table for the content:

Tab	Button Label	Image	Text
2	**No parking first half of month**	e5_noParkingFirstHalf.png	This road sign prohibits parking from the 1st to 15th of the month. However, parking is allowed during the second half of the month in this area.
3	**No parking second half of month**	e7_noParkingSecondHalf.png	This road sign prohibits parking from the 16th to 31st of the month, but parking is allowed during the first half of the month in this area.

If you want to further customize this interaction, don't hesitate to click on the **Custom** category at the bottom of the left column. The available options should be self-explanatory.

20. When done, click on the **OK** button to validate the changes and close the **Configure interaction** dialog.

21. Move and resize the widget so that it nicely fit on the slide.

22. Save the project and use the preview icon to test the new interaction.

The user experience provided by the **Tabs** interaction is very different from the original experience. That being said, this smart learning interaction enables us to deliver the same content and to maintain a high level of interactivity in the mobile-friendly project.

Rollover images

The third and final rollover object of Captivate is the Rollover Image object that is on slide 15 of the project.

To make this content mobile-friendly, we will simply replace the rollover images by standard images. By doing so, we will lose the rollover interactivity, but we will ensure that the same content as in the original version of the project is provided. Perform the following steps:

1. Select the three rollover images of the slide. Notice that their corresponding rollover areas are selected as well.

2. Delete the selected objects.

3. Also delete the rotated text caption at the top-right corner of the slide.

We will now replace the deleted rollover images by standard images:

4. Open the **LIBRARY** panel situated next to the **PROPERTIES** panel.

5. In the **Images** section of the **LIBRARY** panel, select the `priority.png` image.

6. Drag the `priority.png` image from the `Images` folder of the **LIBRARY** panel and drop it next to the **I have the right of the way** text caption.

7. Use the smart guides of Captivate 7 to quickly align the image with the corresponding text caption.

Turning smart guides on and off

The smart guides are these green dotted lines that appear on the stage when you move objects around. These guides are meant to help you quickly align objects together. If you don't see them, make sure the **View | Show Drawing / Smart Guides** menu item is turned on. Smart guides are a new feature of Captivate 7.

8. Also drag the `noPriority.png` image to the right of the second text caption, and the `PriorityRight.png` image to the right of the third text caption. Use the smart guides to properly align these images on the stage.

9. Move all three images to the end of the **TIMELINE** panel, so they appear at the same time as the text captions.

10. In the **Transition** section of the **PROPERTIES** panel, set the **Effect** of the images to **Fade In Only**.

Another look at the HTML5 Tracker panel

With the rollover objects of Captivate removed from the project, all of the issues listed in the **HTML5 Tracker** have been addressed.

1. Go to the **Window | HTML5 Tracker** menu item to open the **HTML5 Tracker** panel.

2. Confirm that the **HTML5 Tracker** panel is now empty.

This, however, does not mean that the job of making this project function correctly in a mobile-environment is over.

Other changes

First, there are a few unsupported features that were (surprisingly) never mentioned in the **HTML5 Tracker** panel.

Second, the changes that we have made to the project in order to make it mobile-friendly require other parts of the project to be updated as well. For example, some of the voice-over narrations are no longer adequate to the current situation.

Dealing with unsupported effects

In *Chapter 2, Creating a Mobile-friendly Interactive Simulation*, we discussed how to use the **EFFECTS** panel to apply engaging visual effects to the objects of Captivate. You discovered that a very small subset of these effects are supported in HTML5.

The effects used in this particular project are all supported in the HTML5 output of Captivate 7, so no extra work is needed from you! However, be aware that if an unsupported effect is used, it does *not* appear in the **HTML5 Tracker** window, because it does not prevent the project to be published anyway. Also, remember that the **EFFECTS** panel of Captivate 7 provides some information about the supported, unsupported, and partially supported effects in HTML5.

Graceful degradation of the unsupported effect

If an unsupported effect is used in a project, it does not mean that it needs to be removed at all costs. Remember that the unsupported effects will simply be ignored in the HTML5 output. This has the following consequences:

- All of the effects will play as intended in the Flash version of our content.

- In the mobile (HTML5) version, the unsupported effects will be ignored. But the way, the objects are organized on the **TIMELINE** panel and the use of the **Fade In** and/or **Fade Out** transitions should be sufficient to provide a more than satisfactory experience to the mobile students while providing the exact same content as in the Flash version.

Sometimes, it is not necessary to reproduce the very same experience on both the Flash and the HTML5 versions. Remember that it is the content that matters the most, and that a slightly less sophisticated experience will not take from the overall learning experience on a mobile device.

Widgets in a mobile-friendly project

Widgets are configurable Flash objects written in action script. They allow third-party developers to expand the functionalities of Captivate. Some widgets (such as the smart learning interactions we discussed previously) are supported in both the Flash and the HTML5 output. However, most widgets are only supported by the Flash technology.

 For more information on HTML5 support for widgets, see the blog post by Tristan Ward a.k.a the Widget King at `http://www.infosemantics.com.au/widgetking/2012/06/new-widget-features-in-captivate-6/`.

In our project, slide 3 contains a button widget that is ignored in the HTML5 output. We will delete this button and replace it with a standard Captivate button as shown in the following steps:

1. Use the **FILMSTRIP** panel to go to slide 3 of the project.

2. Select the **Next** button.

3. Take a look at the topmost area of the **PROPERTIES** panel. Notice that the selected object is an **Interactive Widget**, not a standard Captivate button.

4. Delete this **Next** button.

5. Go to **Insert | Standard Objects | Button,** or use the button icon in the vertical toolbar, to create a new standard button.

6. In the **PROPERTIES** panel, apply the **MFTC-ButtonContinue** style and make sure that the **On Success** action is set to **Go to the next slide**.

7. Move the new button to the location where the **Next** button used to be.

8. In the **TIMELINE** panel, move the button to the end of the slide's **TIMELINE**.

Note that this unsupported widget was never mentioned in the **HTML5 Tracker** panel. As a best practice, you should therefore extensively test the HTML5 output of your projects even if the **HTML5 Tracker** panel shows no issues.

Modifying the voice over narration with the text-to-speech engine

This project uses the text-to-speech engine of Captivate 7 to produce the voice-over sound clips. Because of the changes we made to the project, some of the voice-over narrations needs to be updated.

Loading the speech agents

This exercise requires that you download and install the speech agents of Captivate. These are available as a separate download at http://www.adobe.com/go/Cp7_win32_voices_installer (Windows 32 bits), http://www.adobe.com/go/Cp7_win64_voices_installer (Windows 64 bits), or http://www.adobe.com/go/Cp7_mac_voices_installer (Mac).

1. Use the **FILMSTRIP** panel to go to slide 15.

2. Go to the **Window | Slide Notes** menu item to reveal the **Slide Notes** panel.

The **Slide Notes** panel is where we insert the script for the narration. By default, the **Slide Notes** panel appears at the bottom of the screen, next to the **TIMELINE** panel.

3. Double-click in the second slide note (the one that begins with **Pass your mouse on these situations...**).

4. Change the content of the second slide note to **Take some time to review these road signs, then click on the Continue button**.

5. Click on the **Text-to-Speech** button situated in the upper area of the **Slide Notes** panel, as seen in the following screenshot:.

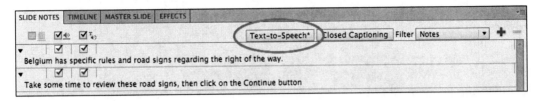

6. At the bottom of the **Speech Management** dialog, click on the **Generate Audio** button.
7. Click on **Yes** to confirm that you want to change the audio of slide 15.
8. When the audio conversion is finished, close the **Speech Management** dialog.
9. Go to the **TIMELINE** panel of slide 15 and move the audio clip so it begins half a second into the slide.
10. Rearrange the timing of the other objects of the slide so they play in sync with the new audio.

After you've completed these tasks, don't forget to save the file.

Testing the HTML5 output

Our mobile version of the Driving In Belgium project is now almost ready for publication. But before you publish, you should test drive the HTML5 output of the project in a compliant web browser.

1. Go to **File | Preview | HTML5 Output In Web Browser** menu item to test the project in a web browser.

Summary

In this chapter, we have converted an existing Captivate project into mobile-friendly content. Basically, this task consists of removing the unsupported objects and replacing them by objects that are compatible in HTML5.

During this process, we discovered that it is not always possible to reproduce the exact same user experience in both Flash (.swf) and HTML5. Remember, it is the content that is the most important part of the project. While converting an existing project to HTML5 we must therefore make sure that the entire content is delivered to each and every student.

Your first task was to recognize the unsupported features. To assist you, Captivate provides the **HTML5 Tracker** panel, a special panel that lists the objects and features that are not supported in HTML5. Remember that some of the unsupported features are not listed in the **HTML5 Tracker** panel. As a best practice, never forget to extensively test the HTML5 output of your project even if the **HTML5 Tracker** panel is empty.

Finally, this chapter gave you the opportunity to discuss some of the greatest features of Captivate, including object grouping, smart shapes, smart learning interactions, advanced actions, and many more.

In the next chapter, we will insert question slides in our project to create a mobile-friendly quiz.

4
Creating a Mobile-friendly Quiz

Quizzes are probably one of the most powerful features of Captivate. By adding question slides to your project, you will be able to measure your student's knowledge, and report the scoring data to a **Learning Management System (LMS)**.

As of Captivate 7, Adobe has succeeded in translating every single Quiz feature into HTML5. Therefore, you can use the quizzes of Captivate 7 with no restrictions, regardless of the project being published in Flash or HTML 5.

In this chapter, you will briefly review the available question types and set up the reporting properties of the Quiz.

Examining the Quiz

While a detailed discussion on Quiz and Question slides is beyond the scope of this book, we will nevertheless take some time to discover the basic features of a quiz.

 A detailed discussion on this subject, as well as a step-by-step tutorial on building the quiz we will use in this chapter, can be found in *Chapter 7, Working with Quizzes* of *Mastering Adobe Captivate 6* by Packt Publishing http://www.packtpub.com/mastering-adobe-captivate-6/book.

1. Browse to your exercises folder and open the drivingInBe_quizStart.cptx file.

2. Navigate to **File | Save As** to save the file as drivingInBe_quiz.cptx.

3. Use the preview icon to preview the entire project. Alternatively, you can navigate to the **File | Preview | Project** menu item.

Pay close attention to the different types of questions, and to the way the student (in this case, yourself) interacts with these slides. Also notice the Quiz Result slide at the very end of the quiz.

4. When you have reviewed the entire project, close the **Preview** window.

5. Repeat step 3 to **Preview** the entire project once again.

During the second preview, you should notice that the question on slide 5 is different than what you saw on the first attempt. This is due to the **Question Pool** and **Random Question** slide present in the project.

Types of question slides

At the heart of the Quiz feature of Captivate are the Question Slides. Captivate supports eight types of Question Slides. Perform the following steps to identify the question types:

1. Navigate to the **Insert | Question Slide** menu item to open the list of supported question types.

The **Insert Questions** dialog box opens and displays a list of the question types that are supported by Captivate.

2. Select the checkbox next to the **Multiple Choice** question type.

3. Open the **Graded** drop-down menu, as shown in the following screenshot:

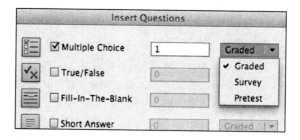

Each question can either be a **Graded** question, a **Survey** question, or a **Pretest** question.

4. Select the checkbox next to the **Rating Scale (Likert)** question type.

Notice that the **Survey** drop-down menu associated with the **Likert** question type is disabled, even if the corresponding checkbox is selected. Unlike the other question types, the **Likert** question can only be a **Survey** question.

5. Click on the **Cancel** button to close the **Insert Question** dialog without inserting any new slide.

Refer to the Captivate help at `http://help.adobe.com/ en_US/captivate/cp/using/WS16484b78be4e1542- 49d8496e13205a3aa39-8000.html` for a complete description of each question type.

We will now take a look at the **FILMSTRIP** panel and see how these questions are implemented in the project:

6. Go to slide 3 in the **FILMSTRIP** panel.

Slide 3 is the first question slide of the project.

7. Next to the **PROPERTIES** and the **LIBRARY** panels, notice the new **QUIZ PROPERTIES** panel. The **QUIZ PROPERTIES** panel is only available while on a question slide.

8. The currently selected question slide is a matching question as mentioned at the very top of the **QUIZ PROPERTIES** panel.

Use the **FILMSTRIP** panel to browse the other question slides of the project while keeping an eye at the top of the **QUIZ PROPERTIES** panel to identify the type of each question.

Question pools and random question slides

The fifth slide of the project is a random question slide.

1. Use the **FILMSTRIP** panel to go to slide 5.

This **Random Question** is linked to the **drivingInBelgiumPool1** Question Pool.

2. Navigate to the **Window | Question Pool** menu item to open the **QUESTION POOL** panel.

By default, the **QUESTION POOL** panel appears at the bottom of the screen, next to the **TIMELINE** and **MASTER SLIDE** panels, as shown in the following screenshot:

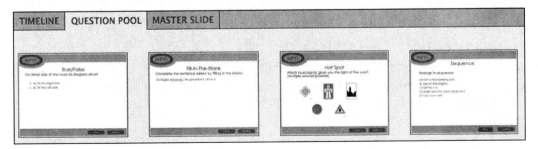

The **drivingInBelgiumPool1** contains four question slides. Slide 5 of the main
FILMSTRIP randomly picks one of these four question slides and displays it
to the student. A single quiz can contain an unlimited number of question pools,
and a single question pool can contain an unlimited number of question slides.

3.   Take some time to browse the four question slides of the **QUESTION POOL**
     one-by-one. Don't forget to keep an eye at the top of the **QUIZ PROPERTIES**
     panel to identify the type of each question.

You now should have a good overview of the question types supported by Captivate.

The quiz results slide

The quiz results slide is automatically generated when the first question slide is
added to the project. It is used to display some feedback to the student about the
outcome of the quiz as shown in the following steps:

1.   Use the **FILMSTRIP** panel to go to slide 8 of the project.
2.   On the right-hand side of the screen, take a look at the **Quiz Properties** panel.
3.   Select the **Quiz Attempts** checkbox and notice how this information is added
     to the slide.
4.   Deselect the **Quiz Attempts** checkbox to return to the initial situation.

While on the quiz results slide, the **Quiz Properties** panel lets us easily choose what
information we want to display to the student.

Touring the Quiz Preferences

To finish examining the original quiz, let's take a quick look at the Quiz Preferences:

1.   Go to the **Quiz | Quiz Preferences** menu item to open the **Quiz
     Preferences** window.

By default, the **Quiz Preferences** window opens on the **Reporting** category.

2.   Navigate to the **Quiz | Settings** category of the **Preferences** window
     (make sure not to click on the **Recording | Setting** category).
3.   Take some time to review the available options, but don't change them.

Notice the **Show Score at the End of Quiz** checkbox. Deselecting this checkbox would
hide the quiz result slide we discussed earlier.

4. Go to the **Quiz | Pass or Fail** category of **Preferences**.

5. Take some time to inspect the options available in this window. They should be, for the most part, self-explanatory.

6. Click on the **Cancel** button to close the **Preferences** window without applying any changes.

You now have a pretty good idea of the large number of options and possibilities offered by the Quiz feature of Captivate.

Taking a look at the HTML5 Tracker

Once again, **HTML5 Tracker** will help us locate the unsupported slides and features (if any) of our project.

Go to the **Window | HTML5 Tracker** menu item to open the **HTML5 Tracker** panel.

In Captivate 7, the **HTML5 Tracker** window shows two unsupported features, as shown in the following screenshot:

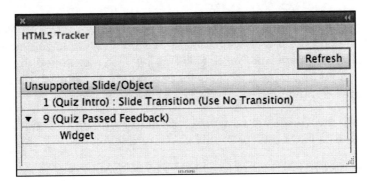

Slide Transitions

The first unsupported feature is a Slide Transition applied to slide 1.

1. Use the **FILMSTRIP** panel to go to slide 1.

2. In the **General** category of the **PROPERTIES** panel, notice that the **Transition** is set to **Wipe**.

3. Go to the **File | Preview | Next 5 Slides** menu item to test the first few slides of the project. Alternatively, you can use the *F10* (Windows) or *command + F10* (Mac) shortcut.

This Preview option uses the Flash technology to render the project so all transitions are fully supported. Pay special attention to the *Wipe* transition at the very beginning of the project.

4. Close the **Preview** window.

5. Navigate to the **File | Preview | HTML5 output in web browser** menu item to test the HTML5 version of the project.

Once again, pay special attention to the transition at the very beginning of the project. Notice that the wipe transition is not rendered in the HTML5 output.

Slide transitions are not supported in HTML5, even in Captivate 7. To deal with this minor incompatibility we have two choices. First, we can leave the slide transition as it is. The HTML5 output looks fine without the transition and the wipe transition nicely enhances the Flash version. The other solution is to remove the transition in the **PROPERTIES** panel to make sure that every student has the same user experience. The choice is yours.

The Certificate widget

The second object listed in the **HTML5 Tracker** panel is the **Certificate Widget** on slide 9. In the previous chapters, we had a discussion on widgets and on the fact that most of them are not supported in HTML5. We also mentioned that the smart learning interactions are, in fact, widgets that are supported in both the Flash and HTML5 output of Captivate.

When it comes to the Certificate widget, Captivate 7 contains a Certificate interaction that can be used to replace the Flash-only Certificate widget:

1. Use the **FILMSTRIP** panel to go to slide 9 of the project.

2. Select and delete the Certificate widget.

3. Go to the **Insert | Interactions** menu item to open the **Select Interaction** dialog box.

4. Select the **Award of Excellence** interaction and click on the **Insert** button.

5. In the left column of the **Widget Properties** window, choose any theme of your liking (in the finished file, we used theme 12).

6. Further customize the certificate as you see fit. One of the possibilities is to double-click the default text to change it. Then, click on the **OK** button at the bottom-right corner of the window.

7. Move and resize the Certificate interaction so it integrates nicely with the other elements of the slide. Don't hesitate to use the new smart guides of Captivate 7 to properly position the interaction on the slide.

With the new Certificate interaction in place, all of the incompatibilities listed in the **HTML5 Tracker** panel have been addressed.

Note that none of these issues were actually related to quizzes. As a matter of fact, with the release of Captivate 7, Adobe has successfully translated the entire set of quiz-related features to HTML5.

Reporting interactions to an LMS

A Learning Management System (LMS) is used to host your e-learning content and deliver it to your students. Most LMSs are deployed on a web server and are able to track the progress and performances of the students. There are many LMSs to choose from. Some are open source solutions and can be used for free, while others are commercial products subject to payment of a license fee.

About LMSs

For more information on LMSs, see http://en.wikipedia.org/wiki/Learning_management_system. For a listing of great open source and commercial LMSs, see http://en.wikipedia.org/wiki/List_of_learning_management_systems.

Captivate is able to send tracking data to virtually any LMS using various standards and methods. As of Captivate 7, all of these methods are now supported in HTML5.

Configuring the reporting options

In this section, we will take the necessary steps to make our mobile-friendly quiz LMS ready!

At the project level

First, we will turn our attention to the reporting options at the project level. This is where you decide on the method that Captivate will use to report the data.

1. Go to the **Quiz | Quiz Preferences** menu item to open the **Preferences** window. The **Preferences** window opens on the **Quiz | Reporting** section.

2. At the top of the **Preferences** window, select the **Enable reporting for this project** checkbox.

3. Open the **LMS** drop-down menu.

The **LMS** drop-down menu is new in Captivate 7. It shows a list of popular LMSs whose compatibility with Captivate has been checked. In this exercise, you will pretend to use the popular open source Moodle LMS.

4. Select the **Moodle** option.

Notice how the other options of the **Quiz | Reporting** Preferences pane are automatically adjusted.

If your LMS is not listed, it means that you'll need to adjust all of these options by yourself, not that you cannot use your LMS with Captivate. One of the main options that you'll need to figure out is the standard your LMS is compatible with.

5. Open the **Standard** drop-down menu and take a look at the available options.
6. When done, make sure you stay on the **SCORM 1.2** standard.

This menu lists the reporting methods and standards available in Captivate.

Most LMSs are compatible with the SCORM, AICC, or Tin Can standard (and sometimes with all of these standards). You should check which standard is supported by your particular LMS before publishing the project.

About SCORM, AICC, and Tin Can

A full discussion on SCORM and AICC is beyond the scope of this book. More information on SCORM can be found at `http://www.adlnet.org/scorm`. More information on AICC can be found at `http://www.aicc.org/joomla/dev/`. More information on Tin Can can be found at `http://tincanapi.com/`.

In this case, you chose the **SCORM 1.2** standard because it is the option to use with the Moodle LMS.

About Moodle

Moodle is one of the most popular open source LMS solutions. For more information about Moodle, see the official Moodle website at `http://www.moodle.org`. Packt Publishing has a wide range of titles available to help you master all aspects of Moodle `https://www.packtpub.com/books/moodle`.

Take some time to inspect the other available options. They should, for the most part, be self-explanatory. Note that the available options depend on the chosen reporting standard.

Creating the SCORM manifest file

In the SCORM specification, the manifest is an .xml file used to describe the SCORM package to the LMS. This manifest file must comply with strict rules and naming conventions in order to be understood by a SCORM-compliant LMS. Captivate makes the creation of the SCORM manifest very simple as shown in the following steps:

1. While still in the **Preferences** window, click on the **Configure** button situated next to the **SCORM 1.2** drop-down menu.

2. In the **Course** category of the **Manifest** window, type:
   - DIB101 in the course **Identifier** field
   - Driving In Belgium in the **Title** field
   - A short description in the **Description** field

3. In the **SCO** category of the **Manifest** window, type:
   - DIB101 in the **Identifier** field
   - Driving In Belgium in the **Title** field.

4. Make sure the **Manifest** window looks like the following screenshot, then click on the **OK** button to validate the changes and close the **Manifest** window.

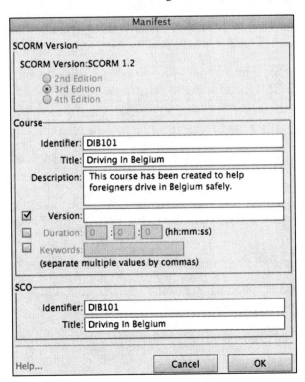

5. Click on the main **OK** button to validate the changes and close the **Preferences** window.

Don't forget to save the file.

At the slide level

Now, we need to decide which interactions we want to report to the LMS. In addition to the question slides, any interactive object in Captivate (Click Boxes, Text Entry Boxes, and Buttons) can be included in a quiz.

Finding the scorable objects

Go to the **Project | Advanced Interaction** menu item to have a list of all the scorable objects of Captivate, that is, all of the objects that can be reported to an LMS.

1. Use the **FILMSTRIP** panel to go to slide 3 of the project.

Slide 3 should be the first question slide of the project.

2. At the bottom of the **Quiz Properties** panel, open the **Reporting** section.

3. Make sure the **Report Answer checkbox** is selected.

This checkbox lets you decide whether to include this particular interaction in the quiz or not. If the checkbox is selected, it is necessary to specify a unique Interaction ID.

The Interaction ID is the name under which this particular interaction will be reported to the LMS. This information is required and must be unique inside of a SCORM package.

4. Change **Interaction ID** to **Match_SpeedLimits**.

To ensure the uniqueness of the Interaction IDs, your best option is to adopt some kind of naming pattern. In this case, the **Match_** prefix identifies a Matching question.

5. Change **Interaction ID** of the remaining question slides of this project. Don't forget the question slides that are in the **drivingInBePool1** Question Pool!

For Random Questions, the Interaction ID is specified on the question slide in the Question pool, while the **Report Answer** checkbox is situated on the Random Question in the main **FILMSTRIP** panel (in your case, on slide 5).

Make sure you assign a unique Interaction ID to each question. Notice that an Interaction ID cannot contain any spaces or special characters.

6. After you've completed assigning unique Interaction ID's, use the **FILMSTRIP** panel to return to slide 2, and select the big gray button situated in the bottom area of the slide.

7. With the Button selected, take a look at the **Reporting** section of the **PROPERTIES** panel.

The `button` object is one of the interactive objects of Captivate. As such, it can be turned into a scorable object and inserted into the quiz. The Click Box and Text Entry Box objects have the exact same capabilities. In your case, you don't want the button to be part of the Quiz, so you will leave the **Include In Quiz** checkbox deselected.

All of the reporting options of your Quiz have been correctly adjusted.
Your mobile-friendly project is now ready for publication.

Summary

In this chapter, you have had a pretty good overview of Captivate's Quiz features. You have discovered the different types of question slides, and you have toured the **Quiz Preferences**.

You also discovered that, as of Captivate 7, quizzes are entirely supported in HTML5. If you are still using Captivate 6 or 6.1, there are a bunch of question slides and reporting options that are not supported. Use **HTML5 Tracker** to identify these question slides.

Finally, you have adjusted the necessary options to turn this mobile-friendly project into a SCORM-compliant package. These adjustments will enable you to easily deploy your Captivate content in any SCORM compliant LMS, and to track the progress and performances of your students. Captivate is also compatible with the AICC and Tin Can standards.

In the next chapter, you will publish your project in order to make it available to the outside world. You will review all aspects of the HTML5 publication and examine the generated HTML files.

5
Publishing a Captivate Project for Mobile

The publishing phase is the last step of the typical Captivate production workflow. By publishing the Captivate project, we make it available to our students.

Traditionally, Captivate projects were published into the Adobe Flash format. The result was a .swf file that could be uploaded to a web server and that was read by the Flash player browser plugin. But the mobile revolution has changed it all. Remember that the Flash player plugin was never supported on the iPad and is not being updated anymore on other mobile device. That's why Captivate 6 has introduced a brand new way of publishing our content. We can now generate an HTML5 web application from an Adobe Captivate project.

In this chapter, you will first get the project ready for publication by exploring the available project preferences and by creating mobile-optimized playback controls. You will then explore various options to publish our project in HTML5 and take a close look at the generated files.

Adjusting the project preferences

Before publishing the project, you will take some time to review the project **Preferences**.

1. Open the HDSB_publish_start.cptx file.
2. Navigate to the **File | Project info** menu item to open the **Project Info** dialog.

The options situated in the **Project** section of the **Preferences** window, marked as **1** in the following screenshot, relate only to the currently open project.

The upper area of the **Project | Information** category, marked as **2** in the following screenshot, allows you to enter information about the project. This information helps make the project searchable and enhances the overall accessibility of the project. This kind of information is called metadata. A metadata is "data about data" (in this case, information about your project).

3. Enter your name and contact information, as well as the name and description of the project.

The bottom part of the **Information Preferences**, marked as **3** in the following screenshot, displays some automatically generated metadata. These metadata cannot be changed, but are very useful to correctly reference your project.

> Some of this metadata is also available in the **PROJET INFO** panel, situated next to the **PROPERTIES** and **LIBRARY** panels.

Make sure the **Project | Information Preferences** looks like the following screenshot before proceeding:

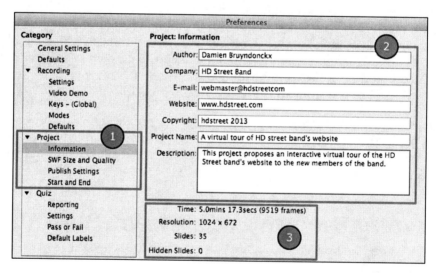

4. Click on the **Project | Start and End** category in the left column of the **Preferences** window.

The upper part of this section of the **Preferences** window contains options that let us decide how the project should start. In the bottom part of the window are the **Project End Options**.

5. In **Project Start Options**, select the **Fade in on the First Slide** checkbox.

6. In **Project End Options**, open the **Action** drop-down menu.

7. Take some time to review the available options then choose **Close Project**.

8. Select the **Fade Out on the Last Slide** checkbox.

9. Take some time to review the other options of the **Preferences** window. Most of them should be self-explanatory.

10. Also take a quick look at the **SWF size and Quality** and the **Publish Settings** sections of the **Preferences** window without changing any of the available options.

11. When done, click on the **OK** button to apply the changes and close the **Preferences** window.

We now have a pretty good idea of the available project preferences. Don't forget to save the project before continuing.

The project skin

The skin of a project is a collection of three elements. These elements are the playback controls, the borders, and the table of contents. By default, these elements appear around the published project when viewed in a web browser or in the **Preview** window of Captivate. In such a case, they add extra pixels to the height and to the width of the project. This can cause problems on mobile devices where the screen real-estate is limited.

In this section, we will use **Skin Editor** to turn off the elements of the Skin:

1. Go to the **Project | Skin Editor** menu item to open the **Skin Editor**.

The **Skin Editor** is divided into two parts. On the left are the options and checkboxes that let us fine-tune each of the three elements of the skin. On the right is a preview of the published project with the skin applied. This preview updates automatically when an option is changed on the left.

Note that at the top of the left column of the **Skin Editor** are three icons which represent the three elements of the skin. You should currently be on the **Playback Control** options, as shown in the following screenshot:

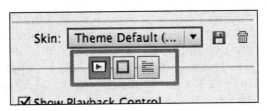

2. Deselect the **Show Playback Control** checkbox.

After a short while, the playback controls are removed from the preview pane on the right, and are replaced by a brownish border. This bottom border was automatically turned on to accommodate the playback controls.

3. At the top of the left column, click on the borders icon (refer to the previous screenshot).

Notice that the border is 30 pixels wide. This matches the height of the playback controls bar that we just turned off. Remember that when we created this particular project, we used one of the iPad presets of Captivate. These 30 pixels increase the overall height of the project. Consequently, the project does not fit an iPad screen anymore. While it is possible to overlay the playback controls so that these 30 pixels do not add up to the overall height of the project, we have decided to completely hide the playback controls instead.

4. Deselect the **Show Borders** checkbox.

Problem solved! Now that the border has been turned off, the height of the project matches the height of an iPad screen in landscape mode again.

5. At the top of the left column of the **Skin Editor**, click on the table of contents icon (refer to the previous screenshot).

6. Select the **Show TOC** checkbox and take a quick look at the preview area to see how the default table of contents is displayed. When done, deselect the **Show TOC** checkbox.

7. Close the **Skin Editor**. Then save and close the file.

All of the elements of the skin have been turned off. The good news is that there are no more extra elements that are adding their extra pixels to the height and width of the project. The bad news is that the student has no more buttons to control the movie. In the HD Street Band project, this is not much of a problem, but in the Driving in Belgium project we would like to provide at least some controls to the student.

Creating mobile-optimized playback controls

Remember that the mobile devices are the touch devices, and that the tip of a finger is much bigger (and therefore, much less precise) than the pointer of a mouse. When designing our custom playback controls, you should make the buttons much bigger than usual. You should also leave a big space around the buttons to help the student hit the tap target. Perform the following steps:

1. Open the `drivingInBe_Publish.cptx` file situated in your exercises folder.

The project you just opened is the Driving In Belgium project of *Chapter 3, Optimizing an Existing Project for Mobile*, plus the quiz of *Chapter 4, Creating a Mobile-friendly Quiz*, at the end.

2. At the bottom of the screen, open the **MASTER SLIDE** panel. If the **MASTER SLIDE** panel is not displayed, go to the **Window | Master Slide** menu item to turn it on.
3. Click on **Content Master Slide** to select it.

The **Content Master Slide** is where you will define your custom playback controls. Therefore, these will be displayed only on the slides that are linked to **Content Master Slide**. This technique allows you to easily decide which slides the playback controls should be shown on.

4. Select the copyright notice situated on the left-hand side of **Content Master Slide**.
5. At the top of the screen, make sure the **Align** toolbar is visible (if not, go to the **Window | Align** menu item to turn it on).

With the copyright notice is selected, only two of the icons of the **Align** toolbar should be available.

6. Click on the **Center horizontally on the slide icon** (it is the first of the two available icons) to place the copyright notice at the center of the slide.

Importing the playback controls

To speed things up, the playback controls have already been designed and are available in a helper file.

1. Open the `helpers/DIB_playbackControls.cptx` file.

This file contains a single slide. At the center of this slide, a group of five smart shapes define the playback controls we will work with. Take some time to inspect the **TIMELINE** panel of this slide to see how these objects are grouped together.

2. Select the playback controls group at the center of the slide and copy it (*Ctrl + C* on Windows or *command + C* on Mac).
3. Return to **Content Master Slide** of the Driving In Belgium project and paste the group (*Ctrl + V* on Windows or *command + V* on the Mac).
4. With the group selected, open the **Transform** section of the **PROPERTIES** panel.

5. Enter an **X** value of 25 and a **Y** value of 550.

The playback controls should now be located at the bottom-left corner of the **Content Master Slide** window, right where the copyright notice used to be.

Defining the playback control's actions

In this section, we will create four advanced actions. These four actions will ultimately be bound to the Success event of each of the four buttons of our custom playbar.

1. Go to the **Project | Advanced Actions** menu item to open the **Advanced Actions** window.
2. In the top-left corner of the dialog, type pauseMovie as the **Action Name**.
3. Double-click in the first line and open the **Select Action** drop-down menu.
4. Select the **Assign** action.
5. Open the **Select Variable** drop-down and select the cpCmndPause variable.

The cpCmndPause variable is a system variable. It means that it is automatically created by Captivate and is always available in any project. It controls whether the movie is paused or not. If the movie is paused, the value of the variable is **1** (for True or Yes). If the movie is not paused, the variable has a value of **0** (for False or No).

6. Open the **Variable** drop-down menu and choose the **Literal** option.
7. Type 1 in the value field and press *Enter*.

The first action should now say **Assign cpCmndPause With 1**, as shown in the following screenshot. In plain English it translates to "Pause the movie".

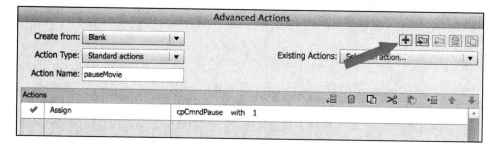

8. Click on the **Save as action** button at the bottom-right corner of the **Advanced Actions** dialog to save the **pauseMovie** action.
9. Click on the **OK** button to acknowledge the successful save of the advanced action.

You will now use the very same procedure to create the remaining three advanced actions we need.

Extra credit

In this extra credit section, you will create the remaining three advanced actions you need to power your new custom playbar. Refer to the following table for details about the actions to create. To create a new action, click on the **+** icon at the top-right corner of the **Advanced Actions** dialog (see the arrow in the previous screenshot).

Action name	Action content
resumeMovie	Asssign cpCmndResume with 1
muteAllAudio	Assign cpCmndMute with 1
unmuteAllAudio	Assign cpCmndMute with 0

Don't forget to save each of these advanced actions and to close the **Advanced Actions** dialog when done.

Binding the actions to the playback controls

All of the pieces of our custom playbar are now ready. The last thing to do is to wire each action to its corresponding button, as shown in the following steps:

1. Return to the **Master Slide** panel and select **Content Master Slide**.
2. Click once on the Playbar to select the entire group. When the group is selected, click on the play icon to select only that icon within the group.
3. In the **Action** section of the **PROPERTIES** panel, open the **On Success** drop-down menu and choose the **Execute Advanced Actions** item.
4. In the **Script** menu, choose the **resumeMovie** action you created in the previous section.
5. Repeat the same sequence of actions to:
    - Bind the **pauseMovie** action to the On Success event of the pause icon
    - Bind the **muteAllAudio** action to the On Success event of the red loudspeaker icon
    - Bind the **unmuteAllAudio** action to the On Success event of the green loudspeaker icon
6. Save the file when done.
7. Use the preview icon, or go to the **File | Preview | Project** menu item, to preview the entire movie and test your new custom playback controls.

If everything works as expected, you can now move on to the core section of this chapter and publish your projects in HTML5.

Publishing the project for mobile

In this section, we will cover the publishing step, which is the third and last step of the typical Captivate production workflow.

Standard HTML5 publishing

You will first publish your project using the standard HTML5 publishing options:

1. Open the `HDSB_publish.cptx` file.
2. Click on the publish icon situated right next to the preview icon in the main toolbar. Alternatively, you can also go to the **File | Publish** menu item.

The **Publish** dialog contains all of the publishing options of Captivate 7, as shown in the following screenshot. In the left column of the dialog, of six icons marked as **1**, represent the main publishing formats supported by Captivate. The area in the center, marked as **2**, displays the options pertaining to the selected format.

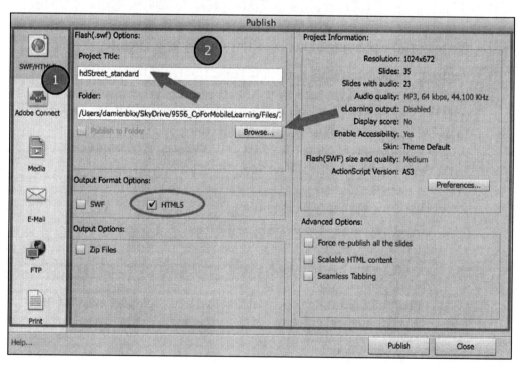

3. Take some time to click on each of the six icons of the left column one-by-one. While doing so, take a close look at the right area of the dialog to see how the set of available options changes based on the selected format.

4. When done, return to the **SWF/HTML5** format, which is the first icon at the top of the left column.

5. Type hdStreet_standard in the **Project Title** field.

6. Click on the **Browse** button associated with the **Folder** field and choose the /published folder of your exercises as the publish location.

7. In the **Output Format Options** section, make sure that the HTML5 checkbox is the only the one selected.

If necessary, adjust the other options so that the **Publish** dialog looks like the previous screenshot.

8. When ready, click on the **Publish** button at the bottom-right corner of the dialog box to trigger the actual publishing process.

This process can take some time depending on the size of the project to publish, and on the overall performances of your computer system. When done, Captivate displays a message, acknowledging the successful completion of the publishing process and asking you if you want to view the output.

9. Click on **No** to close both the message and the **Publish** dialog.

10. Make sure you save the file before proceeding.

Publishing your project to HTML5 is that easy! In the next section, we will use Windows Explorer (Windows) or Finder (Mac) to take a closer look at the generated files.

Examining the HTML5 output

By publishing the project to HTML 5, Captivate has generated a whole bunch of HTML, CSS, and JavaScript files:

1. Use Windows Explorer (Windows) or Finder (Mac) to go to the /published/hdStreet_standard folder of your exercises.

Note that Captivate has created a subfolder in the /published folder we specified as the publish destination. Also notice that the name of that subfolder is what we typed in the **Project Title** field of the **Publish** dialog.

The /published/hdstreet_standard folder should contain the index.html file and five subfolders, as illustrated by the following screenshot:

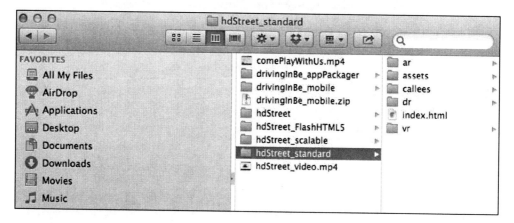

- The index.html file is the main HTML file. It is the file to open in a modern web browser in order to view the e-learning content.
- The /ar folder contains the audio assets of the project. These assets include the voice over narrations and the mouse-click sound in .mp3 format.
- Every single HTML5 Captivate project includes the same /assets folder. It contains the standard images, CSS, and JavaScript files used to power the objects and features that can be included in a project. The web developers reading these lines will probably recognize some of these files. For example, the jQuery library is included in the /assets/js folder.
- The /dr folder contains the images that are specific to this project. These images include the slide backgrounds in .png format, the mouse pointers, and the various states of the buttons used in this project.
- Finally, the /vr folder contains the video assets. These include the video we inserted on slide 2, as well as all of the full motion recording slides of the project.

All of these files and folders are necessary for your HTML5 project to work as expected. In other words, you need to upload all of these files and folders to the web server (or to the LMS) to make the project available to your students. Never try to delete, rename, or move any of these files!

2. Double-click on the index.html file to open the project in the default web browser.
3. Make sure everything works as expected. When done, close the web browser and return to Captivate.

This concludes our overview of the standard HTML5 publishing feature of Captivate 7.

Testing the HTML5 content

Producing content for mobile devices raises the issue of testing the content in a situation as close as possible to reality. Most of the time, you'll test the HTML5 output of Captivate only on the mobile device you own, or even worse, in the desktop version of an HTML5 web browser. If you are a Mac user, I've written a blog post on how to test the Captivate HTML5 content on iOS devices, without even owning such a device at `http://www.dbr-training.eu/index.cfm/blog/test-your-html5-elearning-on-an-ios-device-without-an-ios-device/`.

Publishing an LMS-ready SCORM package in HTML5

We will now publish the Driving In Belgium project as an HTML5 web application. The main difference between this project and the HD Street Band project we just published is the fact that the Driving In Belgium project contains a quiz and a SCORM 1.2 manifest file for data tracking by an LMS. Perform the following steps:

1. Return to the `DrivingInBe_Publish.cptx` file.

2. Use the publish icon or the **File | Publish** menu item to open the **Publish** dialog box.

3. Make sure that the **SWF/HTML5** format is selected in the left column of the **Publish** dialog.

4. Type `drivingInBe_mobile` in the **Project Title** field. Remember that this will become the name of the folder into which Captivate will generate the HTML, JavaScript, and CSS files of our project.

Naming the project

Because the name of the project as it was typed in the **Project Title** field of the **Publish** dialog will be used as the name of the folder into which Captivate will generate the HTML, CSS, and JavaScript files, it is a good idea to name the project according to the naming rules and conventions of the Internet. It means that you should not use spaces and special characters (such as é, è, à, ç, ü, *, !, and so on.) in the title of your projects.

5. Hit the **Browse** button associated with the **Folder** field and choose the `/published` folder of the exercises as the publish destination.

6. In the **Output Format Options** section, make sure that **HTML5** is the only checkbox selected.

7. In the **Output Options** section, select the **Zip Files** checkbox.

8. When ready, click on the **Publish** button.

9. When the publication process is complete, click on the **OK** button to acknowledge the successful completion of the process.

Once again, we will use Windows Explorer (Windows) or Finder (Mac) to examine the generated files.

10. Use Windows Explorer (Windows) or Finder (Mac) to go to the /published folder of the exercises.

The folder should now contain the drivingInBe_mobile.zip file in addition to the HTML5 application we exported earlier. The SCORM specification states that a SCORM-compliant LMS is supposed to be able to receive such a ZIP file, to unzip it, and to properly deploy its content. It means that you can upload the ZIP file to the SCORM-compliant LMS and let the system deploy your e-learning content.

11. Unzip the .zip file to see its content.

Your HTML5 SCORM package contains the same files and folders as those contained in the HTML5 application you explored in the previous section. Some additional files provide SCORM support:

- The index_SCORM.html file replaces the index.html file
- The imsmanifest.xml file is the SCORM 1.2 manifest that you created at the end of the previous chapter. This file must be at the root of the .zip package for the LMS to deploy the content as expected

If you double-click on the index_SCORM.html file, you will get the following JavaScript error message:

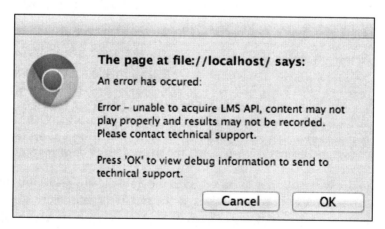

This error is due to the fact that your HTML5 application is trying to talk to an LMS and initialize data tracking. Since you opened the file directly from your hard disk without actually using an LMS, the data-tracking system cannot be initialized and the error is displayed. This is good news for you! It means that SCORM is already at work and that your package has been properly published.

Addressing the multi-screen challenge

One of the biggest challenges of producing content for mobile devices is the wide range of screen sizes that need to be addressed. So far in this book, we have created fixed-sized content. The HD Street Band project has been created based on the size of an iPad screen in landscape mode. The Driving In Belgium project has a fixed width of 800 pixels and a fixed height of 600 pixels, which make it suitable for most screens, but certainly not all.

Adobe Captivate offers two ways to deal with this problem:

The scalable HTML content

The first way is the **Scalable HTML Content** checkbox situated in the **Publish** dialog. Selecting this checkbox makes the content fluid. It means that the content will automatically resize based on the screen it is viewed on (or on the device orientation). Perform the following steps:

1. Return to the HDSB_publish.cptx file.
2. Use the publish icon or go to the **File | Publish** menu item to open the **Publish** dialog.
3. Type HDStreet_scalable as the **Project Title**.
4. Make sure the output folder is still the /published folder of the exercises.
5. Make sure **HTML5** is the only **Output Format** selected.
6. In the **Output Options** section of the **Publish** dialog, make sure the **Zip Files** checkbox is deselected.

Except for the **Project Title**, the current settings should be the same as those we used for the standard HTML5 publication.

7. In the **Advanced Options** section, at the bottom-right corner of the **Publish** dialog, select the **Scalable HTML Content** checkbox.
8. Click on the **Publish** button to start the publication process.
9. When the message appears at the end of the publication process, click on **Yes** to see the HTML5 application in the default web browser.

When the project opens in the web browser, notice how it covers the entire available space. Don't hesitate to resize the browser window as the project plays. You should notice that the project resizes to match the size of the window without ever being distorted.

This is a pretty good and very easy solution to address the multiscreen challenge. Note that at very large sizes, the quality of the image becomes very poor. At very small sizes, it is not possible anymore to read the text or to click (or tap) on a button.

Publishing the project in both Flash and HTML5

Another way to address the multi-device challenge is to publish the project in both Flash and HTML5.

1. Still in the HDSB_publish.cptx file, use the publish icon or the **File | Publish** menu item to open the **Publish** dialog.

Normally, the options of the **Publish** dialog should have been maintained from the last session.

2. Type HDStreet_FlashHtml5 as the **Project Title**.
3. Deselect the **Scalable HTML Content** checkbox situated in the **Advanced Options** section at the bottom-right corner of the **Publish** dialog.
4. In the **Output Format Options** section, select both the **SWF** and the **HTML5** checkboxes.
5. Make sure the other options of the **Publish** dialog are the same as before.
6. Click on the **Publish** button.
7. When the publishing process is over, click on **No** to discard both the message and the **Publish** dialog.

You will now take a look at the generated files.

8. Use Windows Explorer (Windows) or Finder (Mac) to go to the /published/ HDStreet_FlashHTML5 folder of the exercises.

This folder should contain all of the HTML, CSS, and JavaScript files we have already discussed, plus a number of new files as follows:

* The hdStreet_FlashHTML5.swf file is the main Flash file. This is the file that is read by the Flash player browser plugin.
* The hdStreet_FlashHTML5.htm file if the file that triggers the Flash version of the content.

- As before, the `index.html` file is the file that triggers the HTML5 version of the content.

- The `multiscreen.html` file contains a small JavaScript which will redirect the user either to the `hdStreet_FlashHTML5.html` file if on a desktop computer or to the `index.html` file if on a mobile device.

Don't hesitate to give it a try! Double-click on the `hdStreet_FlashHTML5.html` file to test the Flash version, and then click on the `index.html` file to test the HTML5 version. Finally, double-click on the `multiscreen.html` file to see what version of the content you are redirected to. If the Flash version correctly played for you earlier, `multiscreen.html` will default to that version.

Publishing the content in both Flash and HTML5 is an easy way to provide an optimized user experience in almost every situation.

 When publishing both the Flash and the HTML5 version, the student can start the project on a desktop computer using the Flash version, and continue it later on a mobile device using the HTML5 version. In such a situation the student will resume his course on his mobile device right where he left off on the desktop computer, as explained in this YouTube video `http://youtu.be/1oDtOdg3DSk`.

Publishing as a .mp4 video

In *Chapter 1, Creating a Mobile Compliant Screencast*, we used the Video Demo recording mode to create a mobile-compliant screencast. This screencast was a `.mp4` video file. We could upload that file to YouTube (or any other video hosting services) or deploy it on our own web server.

As a matter of fact, any Captivate project can be published as a `.mp4` video file. Keep in mind, though, that the generated video file does not support any kind of interactivity.

It is also important to remember that such a video file can be played back on virtually any desktop and mobile device. Perform the following steps:

1. Still in the `HDSB_publish.cptx` file, use the publish icon or the **File | Publish** menu item to open the **Publish** dialog.

2. In the leftmost column of the **Publish** dialog, select the **Media** format.

3. Open the **Select Type** drop-down menu and choose the **MP4 video (*.mp4)** option.

4. Type `hdStreet_video` as the **Project Title** and make sure that the `publish` Folder still points to the `/published` folder of the exercises.

5. Open the **Select Preset** drop-down menu and take some time to inspect the available presets.

6. Choose the **Video – Apple iPad** preset.

7. Click on the **Publish** button.

Captivate will first generate a `.swf` flash file before using the **Adobe Captivate Video Publisher** to convert the `.swf` file into a `.mp4` video.

8. When the entire process is complete, close the **Adobe Captivate Video Publisher**.

9. Use Windows Explorer (Windows) or Finder (Mac) to go to the `/published` folder of the exercises.

You should see the new `HDStreet_video.mp4` file. Double-click on that file to open the video in the default player (`.mp4`). All of the interactivity is gone!

Summary

Now that the project has been published, we have gone through all three steps of the typical Captivate production workflow. We have also reviewed three typical use cases. The first one was creating a High Definition screencast for both desktops and the mobile devices. The second one was creating a brand new mobile project from scratch. The third one was optimizing an existing project for the mobile output.

We started this particular chapter by exploring the **Project Preferences** and the three elements that make up the project skin. We then used the **Master Slides** and the **Advanced Actions** to create custom mobile-optimized playback controls.

In the second part of this chapter, we have discovered how to publish our content in HTML5, and we have explored the available options.

In the next chapter, we will discuss some of the newest and most advanced mobile features and publishing options of Captivate.

6

The Adobe Captivate
App Packager

In this chapter, we will further explore some of the newest mobile features of Adobe Captivate. These new features are packed in a small AIR application called the **Adobe Captivate App Packager**.

The App Packager brings two new tools in our Adobe Captivate toolbox. The first one is the insertion of **Adobe Edge Animate** animations into a Captivate project. Adobe Edge animate is a new authoring tool from Adobe. It allows you to create interactive animations and to publish these animations in HTML5.

The second one is the ability to use the Adobe Captivate App Packager to transform your HTML5 web applications into native mobile apps for various mobile platforms, including iOS and Android. Your e-learning content will then be available to students through whatever app store is available for each platform, and will install on the mobile device as yet another standalone application.

These two new features are the first ones that have not been derived from an existing Flash feature, but have been made exclusively for HTML5 and mobile devices.

Inserting Edge Animate animations into Captivate

In the first part of this chapter, we will discuss the insertion of Adobe Edge Animate animations into your Captivate project.

About Edge Animate

Adobe Edge Animate is a brand new authoring tool by Adobe. It allows you to create interactive animations using HTML5, CSS, and JavaScript. It is part of the new Adobe Edge suite of tools.

Adobe Edge Animate has a lot in common with Flash Professional. Both applications can be used to create sophisticated web animations. There are also major differences between Flash and Edge Animate. The main difference is the output format of the published (compiled) project.

The primary output format of Flash Professional is the .swf file format, while the primary output format of Adobe Edge Animate is HTML5. This makes Edge Animate animations available to virtually any desktop and mobile browser without the need for a browser plugin.

Adobe Edge Animate is available through the Creative Cloud subscription.

Learning Edge Animate

Joseph Labrecque has written a great book on Learning Edge Animate. Find it on the Packt Publishing website at http://www.packtpub.com/ learning-to-create-engaging-motion-rich-interactivity- with-adobe-edge/book.

Seeing the animations in a web browser

Before you go any further, you will take a quick look at the animations that you will insert in your Captivate project:

1. Open /Animate/RedCross/redCross.html in an HTML5-compliant web browser, such as Google Chrome.

You should see the red cross animation right in your web browser. This animation is much more sophisticated than the ones you have been able to achieve with the **EFFECTS** panel of Captivate.

2. Open /Animate/greenCheck/greenCheck.html in an HTML5-compliant web browser, such as Google Chrome.

Once again, a much more sophisticated version of the green checkmark animation plays in the web browser.

These two animations have the very same size as the Driving In Belgium project (800 pixels by 600 pixels) and have a transparent background.

Seeing these animations in Adobe Edge Animate

If Adobe Edge Animate is installed on your system, feel free to open the corresponding .an files situated next to the .html files. You can then explore these animations from within Adobe Edge Animate.

Getting the project ready

In the next couple of pages, we will replace the existing red cross and green check images of the Driving In Belgium project by their Edge Animate alternatives.

Removing standard animations from the project

The first step of this process is to remove the existing red cross and green check images from the project as shown in the following steps:

1. Open the `drivingInBe_appPackager.cptx` file situated in the exercises folder.
2. Use the **FILMSTRIP** panel to go to slide 6 of the project.
3. Select the green checkmark image and delete it, note that the green checkmark is off stage!
4. Also delete the red cross images of slide 7 and 11 as well as the green checkmark of slide 10.
5. Save the file when done.

You should have removed four images from the project.

Publishing the project in HTML5

The actual replacement of the images by their Edge Animate animations counterparts will take place in the Adobe Captivate App Packager. This application needs a *published* HTML5 Captivate project to begin with, so the next step is to publish the project in HTML5 using the techniques covered in the previous chapter:

1. Use the publish icon, or go to the **File | Publish** menu item, to open the **Publish** dialog.
2. In the leftmost column of the **Publish** dialog, make sure that the chosen format is **SWF/HTML5**.
3. Type `drivingInBe_appPackager` as the **Project Title**.

4. Click on the **Browse** button associated with the **Folder** field, and choose the /publish folder of the exercises package as the publish destination.

5. In the **Output Format Options** section, make sure **HTML5** is the only checkbox selected.

6. All the other checkboxes should be deselected, as illustrated in the following screenshot:

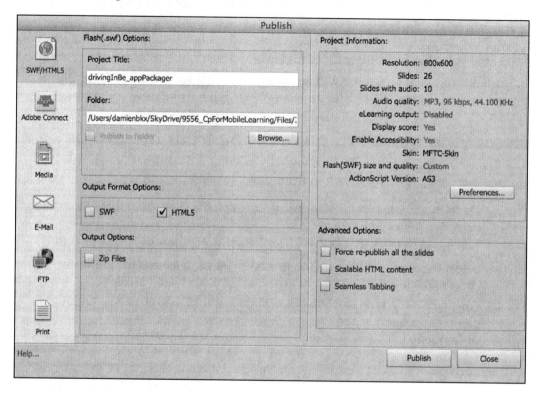

7. Click on the **Publish** button to start the publication process.

8. When done, click on **No** to discard both the message and the **Publish** dialog.

With the project published in HTML5, you can now switch to the Adobe Captivate App Packager for the rest of the process.

The Adobe Captivate App Packager

The rest of the process will take place in the Adobe Captivate 7 App Packager. The Adobe Captivate App Packager is an AIR application that is part of the Captivate 7 bundle.

1. Open the **Adobe Captivate 7 App Packager** application.

The Adobe Captivate App Packager can be found in the /Applications/Adobe folder on a Mac and in the C:\Program Files\Common Files\Adobe\Adobe Captivate App Packager on a Windows PC.

> If you are using the 32-bit version of Captivate for Windows, you should read Program Files (x86) instead of Program Files.

2. Click on the big **Browse** button at the center of the screen.
3. Select the /Published/drivinInBe_appPackager folder of the exercises files. It is the folder where you published the HTML5 project earlier in this chapter.

The Adobe Captivate App Packager loads the **Driving In Belgium** project, as seen in the following screenshot:

As you can see, the interface of this small application looks like a lightweight version of Captivate, with the stage at the center and a set of panels around it. There is a **FILMSTRIP** panel on the left-hand side, marked as **1, in the above screenshot**. On the right-hand side is a stack of four panels, marked as **2**. The topmost panel of the stack is the **IMPORT ANIMATION** panel that we will use to import the Edge Animate files into our project. At the bottom of the screen is another panel, marked as **3**, which gives us access to the publishing options.

 Windows 8 users will see a fifth icon in the bottom panel allowing them to package their application for the Windows Metro platform.

Inserting the Edge Animate animation

We will now use the **Import Animation** panel to import our Edge Animate project into the Adobe Captivate App Packager, as shown in the following steps:

1. Locate the **Import Application** panel in the top-right corner of the screen.
2. Click on the green colored **Eg** icon.
3. Select the `/Animate/greenCheck.oam` file and click on the **Open** button.

An `.oam` file is an Animate Deployment Package. Publishing your animation as an `.oam` file is one of the publishing options found in Edge Animate.

4. Use the **FILMSTRIP** panel on the left to go to slide 6.
5. With the green checkmark animation playing in the **Import Animation** panel, click on the green arrowed **Insert** button, shown in the following screenshot:

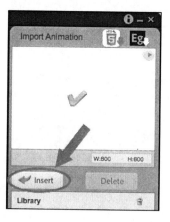

The Edge Animate animation is inserted into the slide. Notice that it is also added to the **Library** panel.

Remember that this animation has the same size as the entire slide and has a transparent background.

6. In the **Transform** panel, set both the **X** and the **Y** coordinates to **0**. This places the animation in the top-left corner of the slide.

7. Still in the **Transform** panel, set the Width (**W**) of the animation to **800** pixels and the Height (**H**) to **600** pixels.

The animation now effectively covers the entire slide.

Extra credit

In this extra credit section, you will repeat the above sequence of actions to import the /Animate/RedCross.oam file into the project and insert it on top of slide 7.

When done, you must insert a second instance of the greenCheck.oam animation on top of slide 10, and a second instance of the RedCross.oam animation on top of slide 11. There is no need to import these animations a second time into the **Import Animation** panel, as they are already present in **Library** panel.

Publishing the updated HTML5 package

Now that we have enhanced the original project with some extra animations, we need to re-publish it. The publishing options of the Adobe Captivate App Packager are grouped in the bottom panel, as shown in the following steps:

1. Click on the first icon, and use the **Browse** button to select the /published folder of the exercises as the publishing destination shown in the following screenshot:

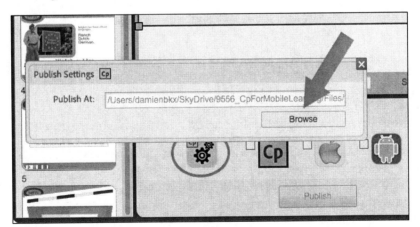

2. Click on the red close button to close the **Publish Settings** window.

3. Select the checkbox associated with the Captivate icon.

This tells the Adobe Captivate App Packager that you want to publish this enhanced project in HTML5.

4. Click on the big **Publish** button situated at the bottom of the panel.

The Adobe Captivate App Packager publishes the enhanced project. When done, a small notification acknowledges the successful completion of the process.

Viewing the enhanced project in a web browser

This is the final step, where everything comes together at last.

1. Use Finder (Mac) or Windows Explorer (Windows) to go to the `/Published/drivingInBe_AppPackager` folder of the exercises.

There are a bunch of extra files present in this folder as compared to those of a standard HTML5 publishing. The enhanced published project resides in the `Captivate` subfolder.

2. Use Finder (Mac) or Windows Explorer (Windows) to go to the `/Published/drivingInBe_AppPackager/Captivate` folder of the exercises.

3. Double-click on the `index.html` file to open it in your default web browser.

Confirm that the imported Edge Animate animations are displayed as expected before moving on.

Leave the Adobe Captivate App Packager open for the next section.

Packaging a Captivate HTML5 project as a native application

When creating content for mobile devices, you basically have two options:

- The first option is to create a mobile web application using HTML5, CSS, and JavaScript. At runtime, a web browser (desktop or mobile) is needed to render this kind of content. The first option is what we have been using throughout the book.

- The second option is to create a Native application. Such an app is distributed through the various App stores available for each mobile platform. It appears as an icon on the mobile device. It is a completely self-contained application that does not need any web browser to render the content.

Each of these two options has its pros and cons.

The mobile web app (the first option) is easy to implement. A single codebase is enough to make the content available on virtually any desktop and mobile browser, making this option a true cross-browser and cross-platform solution. It also enables the web developers to create mobile applications using technologies they already know.

The second option is much more difficult to implement. It requires the knowledge of vendor-specific languages and technologies. An iOS app, for instance, is developed using the Objective-C language, while Android apps are developed using a Java dialect. In other words, each platform needs its own codebase, making it a much more difficult and costly solution. On the other end, these applications can take advantage of all of the super sensors of the mobile devices (the accelerometer, offline storage, the camera, the GPS chip, and many more) giving us tons of new tools and pedagogical opportunities.

 Mobile learning analyst RJ Jacquez has some great articles on the subject on his blog. See `http://rjacquez.com/native-apps-vs-mobile-web-pros-and-cons-infographic/` for good general information on the topic. Don't hesitate to spend some more time on RJ's blog for more.

About PhoneGap and PhoneGap build

PhoneGap is an open source framework for quickly building cross-platform mobile apps using HTML5, JavaScript, and CSS. In other words, PhoneGap lets you create native apps for many platforms using HTML, JavaScript, and CSS!

The real magic of PhoneGap comes from the PhoneGap API. Without getting into too many technical details, this API let you access the super sensors of the mobile device using a JavaScript library. With PhoneGap, you can therefore develop a native-like app using the tools and technologies you already know.

When your app is ready, just upload it to the PhoneGap Build online service to get it compiled for many different mobile platforms (including iOS, Android, Windows phone, Blackberry, and many more).

An excellent introduction article is available on the PhoneGap website at http://phonegap.com/2012/05/02/phonegap-explained-visually/. You can also read the PhoneGap page on Wikipedia http://en.wikipedia.org/wiki/PhoneGap.

PhoneGap and the Adobe Captivate App Packager

The Adobe Captivate App Packager gives you access to the PhoneGap build service allowing you to compile your Captivate HTML5 content into native apps for many different mobile platforms.

Using the App Packager with the PhoneGap build service

It's now time to get our hands dirty and to start experimenting with PhoneGap Build.

The **Adobe Captivate App Packager** should still be open from the previous section. If not, open it and load the Driving In Belgium HTML5 application into the App Packager:

1. In the bottom panel of the Adobe Captivate App Packager, deselect the Adobe Captivate icon checkbox and select the iOS and the Android icons checkboxes, as shown in the following screenshot:

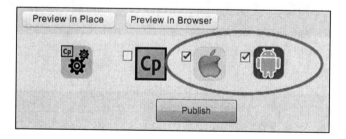

2. Click on the **Publish** button.
3. Use your Adobe ID credentials to log on to the PhoneGap build service.
4. When logged in, select the **Create new** option.

5. Enter `Driving In Belgium` as the **Name** of the application, `1.0` as the **Version** number, and `DIB` as the **Package** name.

6. Make sure the **PhoneGap:Build** window looks like the following screenshot, and hit the **Go** button:

You may be prompted with another window asking for passwords and certificates. For the purpose of this exercise, you can leave all of these fields blank and click on the **Go** button.

 If your application is to be sent out to the Apple App Store, security certificates are mandatory. It is not the case for an Android app. Information about passwords and certificates are available on the PhoneGap build website at `https://build.phonegap.com/`.

7. When the publishing process is finished, click on the **Download** button.

This will take you to the PhoneGap build website where you can download the compiled versions of your application for many different mobile platforms.

Summary

The Adobe Captivate App Packager still needs a lot of improvement! That being said, the features it provides are the very first mobile-only features of Captivate. These features have no equivalent in the Flash world, and as such, can be considered to be the first steps of Captivate in the world of true mobile learning.

At the end of this book, you should have a pretty good idea of what Captivate is up to when it comes to HTML5 publishing and mobile learning. Again, lots of improvements in many areas are still needed to make true mobile learning with Captivate a reality. The huge effort of shifting the core technology of Captivate from Flash to HTML5 is still very much a work in progress.

That being said, some of your projects can probably be published in HTML5 as of today. I hope this book helped you grasp the current state of the HTML5 technology in e-learning and the current capabilities of Captivate 7 in this particular area.

The last point I want to make is that whatever technology or publishing format you use, always have your students in mind. They don't care about the underlying technology and only want a good learning experience. As a teacher, it is exactly what you should provide.

Index

V

About Packt Publishing

Packt, pronounced 'packed', published its first book "*Mastering phpMyAdmin for Effective MySQL Management*" in April 2004 and subsequently continued to specialize in publishing highly focused books on specific technologies and solutions.

Our books and publications share the experiences of your fellow IT professionals in adapting and customizing today's systems, applications, and frameworks. Our solution based books give you the knowledge and power to customize the software and technologies you're using to get the job done. Packt books are more specific and less general than the IT books you have seen in the past. Our unique business model allows us to bring you more focused information, giving you more of what you need to know, and less of what you don't.

Packt is a modern, yet unique publishing company, which focuses on producing quality, cutting-edge books for communities of developers, administrators, and newbies alike. For more information, please visit our website: www.packtpub.com.

Writing for Packt

We welcome all inquiries from people who are interested in authoring. Book proposals should be sent to author@packtpub.com. If your book idea is still at an early stage and you would like to discuss it first before writing a formal book proposal, contact us; one of our commissioning editors will get in touch with you.

We're not just looking for published authors; if you have strong technical skills but no writing experience, our experienced editors can help you develop a writing career, or simply get some additional reward for your expertise.

PUBLISHING

Learning Adobe Connect 9

ISBN: 978-1-84969-416-2   Paperback: 178 pages

Successfully create and host web meetings, virtual classes, and webinars with Adobe Connect

1. Master all the important features of Adobe Connect

2. Utilize Adobe Connect for your mission critical web conferencing needs, independent of the type of user devices

3. A practical guide to effectively use Adobe Connect for small team collaboration or large-scale meetings, presentations, training, and online events

Adobe Edge Quickstart Guide

ISBN: 978-1-84969-330-1   Paperback: 136 pages

Quickly produce engaging motion and rich interactivity with Adobe Edge Preview 4 and above

1. Learn to use Adobe's newest application to create engaging motion and rich interactivity

2. Familiarize yourself with the Edge interface and unleash your creativity through standard HTML, CSS, and JavaScript

3. Add motion and interactivity to your websites using Web standards

4. A quickstart guide for creating engaging content with Adobe Edge

Please check **www.PacktPub.com** for information on our titles

Mastering Adobe Captivate 6

ISBN: 978-1-84969-244-1   Paperback: 476 pages

Create professional SCORM-complaint eLearning content with Adobe Captivate

1. Step-by-step tutorial to build three projects including a demonstration, a simulation and a random SCORM-compliant quiz featuring all possible question slides

2. Enhance your projects by adding interactivity, animations, sound and more

3. Publish your project in a wide variety of formats enabling virtually any desktop and mobile devices to play your e-learning content

4. Deploy your e-learning content on a SCORM or AICC-compliant LMS

Mastering Adobe Premiere Pro CS6 Hotshot

ISBN: 978-1-84969-478-0   Paperback: 284 pages

Take your video editing skills to new and exciting levels with eight fantastic projects

1. Discover new workflows and the exciting new features of Premiere Pro CS6

2. Take your video editing skills to exciting new levels with clear, concise instructions (and supplied footage)

3. Explore powerful time-saving features that other users don't even know about!

4. Work on actual real-world video editing projects such as short films, interviews, multi-cam, special effects, and the creation of video montages

Please check **www.PacktPub.com** for information on our titles

CPSIA information can be obtained
at www.ICGtesting.com
Printed in the USA
FSOW02n2246040516
20069FS